The Four Centuries Between the Testaments

The Four Centuries Between the Testaments

A Survey of Israel and the Diaspora from 336 BC to 94 AD

by

George E. Balla

BIBAL Press
Publishing agency of BIBAL Corporation
Berkeley Institute of Biblical Archaeology & Literature

The Four Centuries Between the Testaments

Library of Congress Cataloging-in-Publication Data

Balla, George Edward.
   The four centuries between the Testaments : a survey of Israel and the diaspora from 336 BC to 94 AD / by George E. Balla.
      p.   cm.
   Includes bibliographical references.
   ISBN 0-941037-27-4 (pbk.) : $7.95
   1. Jews--History--586 B.C.—70 A.D. 2. Judaism--History--Post-exilic period, 586 B.C.—210 A.D. I. Title.
   DS121.65.B35 1993
   909'.04924--dc20
                                          93-39347
                                              CIP

Published by BIBAL Press
P. O. Box 4531
Vallejo, CA 94590

Printed at GRT Book Printing, Oakland, CA

This book is dedicated

to my parents

Rev. George and Elizabeth Balla

who first introduced me to

the world of the Bible

CONTENTS

CONTENTS

MAPS
   The Assyrian Empire
   The Babylonian Empire
   The Persian Empire
   The Alexandrian Empire
   The Ptolemaic Empire
   The Seleucid Empire
   Maccabean Rule
   Hasmonean Rule
   The Roman Empire
   Herodian Rule

FOREWORD

Christians, for the most part, are familiar with the concepts of Old and New Testaments, since Sunday School education has acquainted them with stories of the important biblical characters and events. They may even have gained a historical framework into which they can place those characters and events. A few may be able to locate geographical sites on a biblical world map.

But hardly any would gain a knowledge of the periods and events which took place between the Old and New Testaments unless they had taken a college survey course in religion, or had read interpretative works on the Apocrypha of the Old Testament. Many may not have even possessed a Bible with the Apocrypha in it unless they owned a "study Bible."

A knowledge of the history which connects the Old and New Testament periods is to be found primarily in Josephus's historical works and I & II Maccabees, two apocryphal books. There have been modern works on the subject, some of which are in the bibliography at the end of this book. But at present there are no works currently in print which lay out the intertestamental period, combining history, geography, and theology. George Balla's work has been meticulously written, and will be a tremendous help for the serious student who wishes to see the reasons for the development of New Testament history, culture, and institutions. He has investigated Josephus, the Maccabees, and other primary and secondary sources to present an overview of the intertestamental period, a period that at its beginning has a paucity of sources upon which one can draw, but at its end has an "embarrassment of riches" in terms of information available.

After a student has digested the contents of this book, reading through the Apocrypha will be much more meaningful, especially a modern version of it which has explanatory prefaces and historical notes, such as contained in *The New Oxford Annotated Bible with the Apocrypha.*

I commend Dr. Balla for making available this work for use by individuals and study groups. It will be an extremely helpful introduction to a period full of surprises and challenges. Several years ago, I taught an adult Sunday School class in this area. We would have had an easier time if we had had this work as a text, but the overwhelming response to the subject was one of excitement and increased understanding of the background of the New Testament. The institutions and religious parties of the New Testament which are not mentioned in the Old Testament (Sanhedrin, synagogue, Pharisee, and Sadducee) were given meaning, and a new understanding of their role and function. An important window on the biblical world had been opened, and the members of the class were very appreciative. This, too, can be your experience as you begin an exciting study of the intertestamental era.

Glenn A. Koch
Professor of New Testament Studies
Eastern Baptist Theological Seminary

PREFACE

This book is written for the person who has little or no knowledge of the intertestamental years, yet wishes to have a brief overview of some of the key events of that time. There are many fine scholarly books on this subject; yet many either presuppose some competence in biblical or intertestamental history, or are so extensive as to discourage the beginner. My hope is that this book will serve as a map, giving a general orientation to the intertestamental landscape, and that after reading this, you will want to read further on the subject.

The idea for this book came about while reading a tantalizing statement by St. Paul, one which evoked a question in my mind. The statement was in his letter to the Galatians which reads, "But when the fullness of the time was come, God sent forth his Son, made of a woman, made under the law" (Gal 4:4).

The question that statement raised was "Why was that particular moment in time the right time for the birth of Jesus?" I realized that I knew little of the events which preceded Jesus' birth nor of the developments in Jewish life during the four hundred years between the testaments. That ignorance on my part set in motion a desire to become familiar with the political and religious developments of the intertestamental era in hopes of finding the answer to my question. The reader may wish to read this book in light of that question also.

I want to thank some people who helped me in the process of developing this book. I first presented some of the material to the Single Adult Fellowship class at the First Baptist Church of Pomona, California. Their interest in, and responsiveness to this material was rewarding and planted the idea that, if presented in book form, others might also be interested. Dr. David A. Hubbard, former president of Fuller Theological Seminary in Pasadena, California, and noted biblical scholar, read the first draft and suggested helpful improvements. Dr. Duane L. Christensen, professor of Old Testament studies at the American Baptist Seminary of the West and president of the Berkeley Institute of Biblical Archaeology and Literature (BIBAL) in Berkeley, California, read the text, made valuable corrections, and encouraged me to pursue possible publication of the book. Dr. Glenn A. Koch, professor of New Testament studies at Eastern Baptist Theological Seminary in Wynnewood, Pennsylvania, carefully read the text and gave excellent recommendations for strengthening the material. He also graciously consented to write the foreword. Dr. William R. Scott, director of BIBAL Press, very kindly added his support to this project, made important recommendations as to the content and organization of the book, and saw it through to its conclusion in an able fashion. I would also like to thank Mr. Dale Liid who prepared the maps for publication. None of the above mentioned scholars, however, is to be held accountable for the final version of this book; it solely reflects my own understanding of the intertestamental years.

Lastly, I want to thank Shirley Sargent, who was my secretary and who waded through hand-written pages to produce the first cohesive draft. Her positive reactions to the material as she typed it meant a great deal. Joy Hunt patiently listened to the material of this book and reacted to it from a layperson's perspective, helping me focus my ideas more clearly. Her support and encouragement were keenly felt. To all who had a part in helping me see this project through, I say a sincere "Thank you."

1

THE GEOPOLITICAL BACKGROUND
The Ancient Near East from David to Alexander

To help the reader relate events of the intertestamental era to those of biblical history, we will begin with the more familiar political events in Jewish life commencing with king David and continuing through the exile. From that vantage point, we will then move into the intertestamental era, showing how it was a vital link in the chain of Old and New Testament history.

Israel, Judah, and the Assyrians
(1000 BC — 612 BC)

Key People:

> **David**, king of Israel and Judah
> **Solomon**, king of Israel and Judah
> **Ahaz**, king of Judah, the southern kingdom
> **Isaiah**, prophet from Judah
> **Tiglath-pileser III**, ruler of the Neo-Assyrian Empire
> **Hoshea**, puppet king placed on Israel's throne by
>   Tiglath-pileser
> **Sargon II**, ruler of the Neo-Assyrian Empire

Key Dates:

> 722/21 BC   conquest of Israel and incorporation into the
>   Assyrian Empire
> 612 BC   conquest of Nineveh, Assyria's capital
> 605 BC   rise of the Neo-Babylonian Empire

Summary:

Under the reigns of kings David and Solomon, the Israelites gained a degree of unity they had not known before. Prior to this, they were divided along tribal lines as well as between north and south. The unity achieved under David and Solomon created in Israel a period of time some refer to as Israel's "Golden Age." That unity brought prosperity and strength to the nation. However, because the nation declined into idolatry and social injustice under Solomon's rule, God decreed that it would suffer division and conquest. Following Solomon's death, the division came about with several tribes forming the northern kingdom, Israel, whose capital was eventually Samaria. Three of the tribes formed the southern kingdom, Judah, whose capital was Jerusalem. Israel continued in sin and refused to heed the words of repentance spoken of by the prophets, a refusal which issued in tragic consequence — conquest by Assyria. That conquest set in motion centuries of foreign domination over Palestine. Assyria's rule lasted one hundred years until the Babylonians and Medes joined forces to conquer it. The Babylonians gained dominance over the fertile crescent and eventually sent Judah into exile.

The intertestamental era, the four hundred years separating the Old Testament from the New, is a period of time not well known to many readers of the Bible. Events of that period, however, naturally evolved from the conditions which existed in Palestine during the closing centuries of the Old Testament period. To show that development we will begin our narrative with the reigns of kings David and Solomon (1000 – 922 BC).

David had already been king of Judah for seven years when he managed to form a unified kingdom out of what had been a loose federation of Israelite tribes. These tribes had known inter-group conflict and war and were already broadly divided between north and south. Under his skillful leadership the nation experienced growth and prosperity, maintaining their freedom to worship God as they chose.

Following David's death, one of his sons, Solomon, became king. Israel's prosperity continued under Solomon who began his rule asking for divine wisdom—a prayer which God answered and to which he added the benefit of great wealth (1 Kgs 3:5-14). Solomon's greatest accomplishment was the building of the Jerusalem temple which his father had envisioned.

In time Solomon changed—a change which had dire effects on the nation. He undertook massive building projects which required heavy taxation of the people. Because of entanglements with the Phoenicians, he was forced to give up some land to their king, Hiram—an action which angered many Israelites. Solomon married 700 wives and had 300 concubines, many of whom were from foreign lands. They brought their native gods and goddesses and worshiped them, a practice Solomon and others also began to follow. Because of these and other situations, God, through his prophets, warned that the nation would suffer division and conquest.

Following Solomon's death, his son Rehoboam became king and the words of the prophets came true. The nation which David forged into a unity split in two. The northern tribes were known as Israel and initially had their capital in Tirzah. Nearly fifty years later, they founded the magnificent city of Samaria and made it their capital. The three southern tribes were known as Judah and retained the capital at Jerusalem.

For almost two hundred years these two kingdoms were in frequent conflict, with consequences devastating for both. During those years Israel prospered, but sunk low into idolatry and social injustice. Prophets such as Amos (750 BC) cried out against those sins, warning that the nation would be conquered if it did not turn from them. These cries went unheeded and, as warned, Israel fell at Assyria's hands within twenty-five years.

Assyria had a long history going back to at least 1900 BC by the time it came into conflict with Israel. It had gone through various stages of power and decline over those centuries and was known as a military society with many feared leaders coming from its ranks.

At the time it conquered Israel, Assyria was beginning a new ascent to power. It controlled Babylon and much of the "fertile crescent." Egypt was also on the rise in power and both nations had dreams of expansion and conquest. The unconquered lands of Palestine were a natural object of interest and Assyria focused its sights on acquiring them. The people of these lands, however, were not willing to let Assyria gain control of them. Thus the stage was set for numerous battles over the next decade.

One of the kingdoms which sought to resist the power of Assyria was Damascus, led by its king, Rezin. He worked to form a coalition including Israel, Edom, Gaza, and Ashkelon, but not Judah, which was then pro-Assyrian.

When Damascus and Israel were not able to persuade Judah to join them in resisting Assyria, they turned against Judah, attacked it and sought to place their own choice of ruler on its throne. Their plans failed as Tiglath-pileser then turned to Israel, taking some of its land and leaving it as a small city state consisting only of the hills of Ephraim around Samaria. Then he placed his choice of king, Hoshea, on Israel's throne. Following that defeat, many Israelites were deported to lands controlled by the Assyrians.

Soon after this initial conquest of Israel, Tiglath-pileser died and two kings followed in quick succession, the second being Sargon II. Hoshea, influenced by Egyptian counsel, refused to pay the required tribute (tax) to Assyria. This angered the Assyrian king, who mounted a full scale attack against Israel, destroying Samaria. He then deported thousands of Israelites to various lands of the empire. These came to be known in popular lore as the "ten lost tribes of Israel," for they never returned to their homeland. In their place Sargon brought peoples from Babylonia and Syria who intermarried with those who had remained in Israel. Their descendants came to be known as the Samaritans (2 Kgs 17:24-29). Thus the prophetic warnings came true in 722/721 when Assyria defeated Israel and incorporated it into its provincial system. With that defeat Israel ceased to exist as a nation. Assyria continued its dominance for almost a century, adding other lands to its holdings.

In time the Assyrian Empire began to weaken. Internal conflict, assassinations, and the difficulty of administering its large holdings all contributed to its eventual fall. Nations which once were subject to it saw this weakness and separated themselves from it—some even daring to attack it. Two of the nations which were emboldened to attack were the Medes and the Babylonians. The Median leader, Cyaxares, joined forces with the Babylonian king, Nabopolassar, in 612 BC and captured Nineveh, Assyria's capital. That marked the end of the once powerful Assyrian Empire and signaled the rise of Babylon as the dominant power in Syria-Palestine. The Medes went their separate ways after the conquest of Nineveh and concentrated on capturing other lands. Egypt made one final attempt to acquire some of the former Assyrian territory, but the Babylonians defeated them at Carchemesh in 605 BC and drove them out of Syria-Palestine. For the next sixty years Babylon controlled major portions of the Near East.

Though the Neo-Babylonian Empire existed for only seventy-five years, these were critical years for the Jews as Judah fell to the Babylonians and its people suffered the infamous seventy year exile in Babylon. With Babylon's rise it would be Judah's turn to learn that the words of the prophets were true: if they did not turn from their sins God would permit their conquest, just as had happened to Israel.

The Neo-Babylonian Empire
(612 BC — 539 BC)

Key People:

> **Nabopolassar,** Chaldean/Babylonian king who, along with the Medes, defeated the Assyrian Empire
>
> **Nebuchadnezzar,** Nabopolassar's son who succeeded to the Babylonian throne
>
> **Jehoiachin,** king of Judah taken prisoner by Nebuchadnezzar (2 Kgs 24:10-17; 2 Chr 36:9-10)
>
> **Zedekiah,** placed on the throne of Judah by Nebuchadnezzar

Key Dates:

> 612 BC   fall of Assyrian Empire and rise of Babylonian Empire
>
> 597 BC   beginning of fall of Jerusalem
>
> 587/86 BC fall of Jerusalem and beginning of Babylonian exile
>
> 539 BC   fall of Babylonian Empire and rise of Persian Empire

Summary:

Under the command of Nabopolassar, the Chaldean/Babylonian king, and Cyazares, the Median king, the Assyrian Empire was defeated and the Neo-Babylonian Empire spread across Syria-Palestine. Nebuchadnezzar became leader of the empire and sent the Jews into exile. During the exile the Jews gained a new and deeper understanding of their faith which helped shape it as a world religion. Within seventy-five years the Persians defeated the Babylonians and emerged as the dominant power in the Near East. Under Persian rule the Jews were permitted to return to their homeland. Many chose to remain in Babylon, but a "remnant" returned to rebuild Jerusalem.

The second great civilization of this period in the ancient Near East was Babylonia. It was located between the Tigris and Euphrates rivers in present-day southern Iraq. Archaeological evidence shows that this area was inhabited as early as 5000 BC. At different times it or the land to its south has been called by various names such as Sumeria, Shinar, Akkad, and the land of the Chaldeans.

The Babylonian region had gone through at least eight political stages from its earliest days until the close of the Old Testament. During these stages it had known both self-rule and domination by neighboring nations, including Assyria. Just prior to the time we are now considering, Babylon (the capital city of Babylonia) had been subject to the influence of Assyria. But when it saw an opportunity, it joined forces with the Medes and conquered its northern neighbors. The greatest figure of that period in Babylon was Nebuchadnezzar who ruled for more than forty of the empire's seventy-five years.

Though Babylon was not always a powerful nation, it produced at least two important personalities still known around the world today. About 1900 BC Abraham, the father of the nation of Israel, came from there. Most people also know of Hammurapi, the ruler who lived some two hundred years after Abraham and produced the famous legal document known as the Code of Hammurapi.

As noted in the previous section, Assyria began to weaken due to internal conflicts and the splintering off of nations from its empire. The Chaldean/Babylonian king, Nabopolassar, joined forces with the Medes and defeated the Assyrians—a victory which ultimately made Babylon the dominant power in Syria-Palestine. Six years later his son, Nebuchadnezzar II, succeeded him. Under the new king's brilliant leadership the empire grew in size, power, and splendor.

During that period Judah was partially independent of Babylon; but, through a series of poor political decisions, eventually fell completely to it, much as Israel earlier had fallen to Assyria. Judah's fall began in 597 BC when its king,

Jehoiachin, was persuaded by the Egyptians to stop paying the tax Nebuchadnezzar levied against him. Egypt had tried several times to thwart the advances of the Babylonians and were attempting with this plot to add more confusion to the existing political picture. However, heeding the counsel of the Egyptians only brought disaster to Judah. Nebuchadnezzar was angered by the decision not to pay the tax and marched against Jerusalem in 597 BC and captured it. He then placed his own choice for king, Zedekiah, on the throne.

Once again the earlier scenario was replayed. The Egyptians persuaded Zedekiah to withhold Nebuchadnezzar's tribute, a decision which naturally angered the Babylonian king. This time the consequences were disastrous. Nebuchadnezzar marched against Jerusalem and destroyed it. The biblical account of that attack is recorded in 2 Kings 24.

For almost three years the Babylonian soldiers hammered at the massive city walls. They cut off the supply of food and water, causing many of Jerusalem's people to die of starvation. Some of these even committed suicide rather than face the uncertainty of what exile could mean. Others fled to different lands, notably Egypt, and began rebuilding their lives there.

When the Babylonian army finally broke through the city walls, they demolished them and burned and razed the temple, as well as most of Jerusalem. The precious golden vessels of the temple were carried back to Babylon along with other valued items. Some believe that it was during this invasion that the sacred Ark of the Covenant was lost. Nebuchadnezzar's policy was to take the choicest citizens of the land back to his homeland. During this first deportation, eighteen thousand were carried into exile a thousand miles from their homeland. Thus, in 587/586 BC the unimaginable had happened: Jerusalem was destroyed and many were taken into exile. The prophecies which had been spoken regarding Judah had come to pass: because of their sins they would be conquered.

The exile in Babylon had a mixed and profound effect on the Jews. For some, God's permission in allowing this tragedy was too great to bear and in their disillusionment they lost their faith. Others adjusted to their new homeland, married, raised families, began businesses, and even served in the government. A remnant, however, who cared deeply for their faith, agonized over the meaning of the exile. They were taught and inspired by prophets such as Isaiah, Jeremiah, and Ezekiel and from them forged a new and deeper faith. When they returned to Jerusalem seventy years later, they brought these new convictions and incorporated them into their religion, making it stronger than before.

They met in homes and small groups during the exile to study, pray, and understand the implications of their new-found insights. From this activity was born the synagogue, which continues as the Jews' main religious institution to this day throughout the world.

Five important new convictions emerged during the exile:
1. God was not confined to the temple in Jerusalem but could be worshiped anywhere.
2. He loved all people of the world and not the Jews alone.
3. He one day would write his laws on the hearts of all people.
4. His kingdom would come one day and he would rule the world eternally in righteousness.
5. The Messiah (God's anointed leader) who brought the kingdom would be a suffering and serving ruler.

These thoughts were new to the Jews and among other things served to make Judaism a world religion, not just a national one. Through this exile, the Jews also learned more clearly that they were to be a "light to the Gentiles" (Isa 42:6; 49:6). Armed with these new convictions, the remnant waited for the exile to end so that they could move forward in their renewed relationship with God.

After the forty year rule of Nebuchadnezzar, a series of ineffective kings governed the empire for about twenty years. Persia saw this weakness in the Babylonian Empire and moved against it, easily destroying it in 539 BC. Persia then released the Jews from Babylon and assisted them monetarily and with personnel in their return to Jerusalem. Persia (now Iran) became the center of a new empire.

The Persian Empire
(539 BC — 331 BC)

Key People:

Cyrus II, ruler of the Persian Empire who freed the Jews from Babylon

Jeremiah, prophesied the downfall of Babylon

Isaiah, prophesied Persia's conquest of Babylon

Ezra, Jewish leader who aided Jews who had returned from the exile

Nehemiah, Jewish leader who aided the Jews in rebuilding Jerusalem

Artaxerxes I, last Persian ruler mentioned in the Old Testament

Darius III, last ruler of the Persian Empire

Alexander the Great, Macedonian ruler who defeated the Persian Empire

Key Dates:

539 BC	Persian Empire defeated Babylon
538 BC	Jews began to return to Jerusalem and restore the city
515 BC	temple restoration completed
331 BC	Alexander the Great conquered the Persian Empire

Summary:

The Persians defeated the Babylonians and allowed the Jews to return to their homeland. A remnant returned while many remained in Babylon and others went to Egypt or other parts of the world. The Persians aided the Jews in restoring their city by giving them money and people to assist. The Jews were under the rule of the Persians but were treated reasonably well by them. Little is known of Jewish life from the end of the Old Testament record (Ezra's mission, early 4th century BC) until 331 BC when Alexander the Great conquered Darius III and the Persian Empire. The Old Testament ends with Persian rule of the Jews.

During the two hundred year existence of the Persian Empire, two important eras came to an end. The first was the end of the Old Testament story with the record of the return of the Jews to Jerusalem from their Babylonian exile. The second was the end of what is commonly called "ancient history" and the beginning of "modern history." This new period was ushered in by the Macedonian, Alexander the Great, when he conquered the Persian Empire.

Most of what is known about the lives of the Jews during the Persian era comes to us from Old Testament books such as Ezra, Nehemiah, Daniel, Esther, and some minor prophets. Those works tell of the struggle the Jews faced as they rebuilt the homeland they had been away from for seventy or more years. Persian records of the Jews during that period are almost non-existent.

It is believed that life for the Jews who remained in Babylon during Persian rule was relatively peaceful. Several thousand chose to live there rather than return to Jerusalem, for life in Babylon was all they knew. The prospects of returning to a demolished Jerusalem and beginning again were too difficult for many to face.

At the end of the Babylonian exile the Jews fell into one of three groups:

1. Those who chose to remain in Babylon under Persian rule.
2. Those who migrated to other parts of the world (the "dispersion"). Many migrated to Egypt during the fall of Israel in 722/21 BC and at the fall of Jerusalem in 587/86.
3. The remnant which returned to Jerusalem.

Each of those groups slowly developed a distinctive style of Judaism which at times was in conflict with those who believed that all of them should be like the Jerusalem Jews. How those differences affected the various groups will be addressed later.

When Persia became the dominant empire, it was young compared to Assyria or Babylonia, having begun about 700 BC. Its first great presence in history came in 559 BC when Cyrus II was its powerful leader. He began by defeating the Medes and then marched against Babylon capturing it without a fight in 539 BC. With that conquest Cyrus established himself as the new world leader. In time the Persian Empire became the largest empire up to that time, with boundaries extending from Egypt almost to India. From its capital in Susa it governed about one million square miles. The prophet Jeremiah foretold the downfall of Babylon (Jeremiah 50) and the prophet Isaiah foretold that Cyrus the Persian would be God's instrument in delivering the Jews from the hand of Babylon (Isa 45:1).

Cyrus's first act was to liberate all people whom the Babylonians had exiled to various lands and to aid them in returning to their homeland. He believed that his vast empire would be easier to manage if the people were content in their own lands. His policy proved to be wise, for his empire remained relatively calm during its two hundred year existence.

Cyrus further ordered that all the religious items which Nebuchadnezzar had stolen were to be returned to their rightful owners. This meant that the treasures taken from the temple in Jerusalem were returned. In addition to this, Cyrus gave the Jews money and people to help them rebuild their city and temple.

The Jews who returned to Jerusalem from Babylon returned in various stages. The first to begin the thousand mile trek back to Jerusalem did so with high hopes of reestablishing their homeland and religion. The new convictions they gained while in exile burned brightly as they believed that God was going to inaugurate his kingdom and rule the world in righteousness from Zion (Isa 46:9-13). From this conviction, messianic expectations were born and continued through the intertestamental era, coming to a climax in the first century AD.

Those first returning Jews were not ready for the sight which greeted them. The city they left behind seventy-five years ago was in shambles. The burned out temple, the torn down walls, the wild vegetation, animals running in the streets, and the poor living in makeshift dwellings, all brought back memories of the terrible destruction by the Babylonian army. Their hearts sunk as they contemplated the task of rebuilding; yet it had to be begun.

God raised up strong leaders such as Ezra and Nehemiah who led the rebuilding in four steps:

1. The altar was rebuilt first. This enabled the Jews to resume the long-stopped practice of offering sacrifices to God (Ezra 3:1-3).
2. The foundation of the temple was laid and the temple completed later (Ezra 3:6-10).
3. The walls around Jerusalem were rebuilt — walls which provided protection from invading groups as well as wild animals (Nehemiah 3-4).
4. The law was reintroduced and became the foundation of their lives (Nehemiah 8).

The long process of rebuilding the walls of Jerusalem and the temple began in 538 BC and was completed in 515 BC.

The Old Testament ends somewhere in this period, probably in the reign of the Persian king, Artaxerxes I, who appears to be the last king mentioned. His rule lasted from 465 BC until 424 BC. From then until Alexander the Great conquered the Persian Empire in 331 BC, little is known of the day-to-day life of the Jews either in Babylon or Jerusalem. Though Persia never gave Palestine its independence, it ruled the Jews in a benevolent manner and permitted them considerable freedom in exercising their lives and religion according to the dictates of their own laws.

After Cyrus died in 530 BC, the Persian Empire underwent periods of loss and restored greatness for almost two hundred years. As had happened to other empires before, it eventually began to weaken because of court intrigues, assassinations, rebellions, and other destructive events. Looming on the horizon was a brilliant young general, Alexander of Macedonia. The calm Persian life was about to be changed for the Jews, for Alexander would introduce Greek ways into the nations he conquered. This change was to tragically affect the Jews for centuries to come.

2
POLITICAL DEVELOPMENTS
IN THE INTERTESTAMENTAL ERA

With the coming of Alexander the Great, the period known as the intertestamental era began. His goal of promoting Greek culture (Hellenism) was to have a profound and lasting effect on the four centuries of the intertestamental era in terms of politics, social life, and religion.

Alexander the Great
(336 BC — 323 BC)

Key People:
> **Philip II**, king of Macedonia who defeated the Greek city states
>
> **Alexander the Great**, Philip's son and ruler of the Greek world
>
> **Aristotle**, Greek philosopher who planted the love of Greek culture in Alexander
>
> **Darius III**, Persian ruler, defeated by Alexander in conquest of the empire

Key Dates:
338 BC	Philip defeated the Greek city states
331 BC	Alexander defeated the Persian Empire
323 BC	Alexander's untimely death

Summary:

King Philip II of Macedonia defeated the Greek city states, setting the stage for his son's conquest of the Persian Empire. Alexander was raised in a royal household and tutored by the famed Greek philosopher Aristotle, who planted in him a love for Greek culture. In all the lands that Alexander conquered he made Greek culture (Hellenism) a required element of his rule. He believed it was the highest expression of human achievement and was necessary to govern his vast empire in a unified manner. Some of the later rulers forced Greek culture, including its religious aspects, on the Jews. This caused much bloodshed and turmoil for the Jews for three hundred years as they refused to worship Greek and Roman gods. Alexander ruled for only twelve years, but his legacy of Hellenism, continued by his successors, plagued the Jews for many generations. With his rule the intertestamental era began.

In the previous three sections our attention was focused on three Near Eastern civilizations which played major roles in Jewish history: Assyria, Babylonia, and Persia. In this section we will enlarge the picture and include Europe. This will be done because of the roles which King Philip II of Macedonia and his son Alexander played in Jewish history. Alexander, taking control of the Macedonian/Greek throne following his father's assassination, conquered both Near Eastern and European nations.

In 338 BC Philip led his troops against the Greek city states and defeated them. Following that victory, he united the many small Greek states — something other leaders had been unable to do. Unifying those forces enabled him to mobilize the Greek army, and together with his Macedonian troops, to gather a formidable military machine. From that position of strength, he began to fulfill his quest of conquering new lands. His goal was short-lived, however, for he died at the hands of an assassin. His death elevated his twenty year old son, Alexander, to the Macedonian/Greek throne.

As a young person Alexander received the best that wealth and position could offer, including the privilege of being personally taught by Aristotle, the famed Greek philosopher. By Aristotle's time the zenith of Greece's glory was passing. The legendary names of Socrates and Plato dominated the previous century as had its famed architecture, athletics, arts, and culture. Aristotle was able to impart Greece's glory to Alexander who passionately absorbed every detail of it. His love for Greek culture infused his later military and political accomplishments.

Following his father's death in 331 BC, Alexander became the leader of the Greek armies. Few could have guessed that the youthful Alexander would prove himself to be a military genius. He devised new weapons and tactics which enabled him to defeat all enemies as he marched across the world. At the time of his death he had conquered lands from Asia Minor and Egypt to India and ruled more territories and peoples than had any previous ruler.

He continued his father's vision of world conquest, first moving his troops south along the Mediterranean coast capturing Syria, Palestine and Egypt. He then attacked Darius III, the Persian ruler. Darius believed that he would be able to dispose of Alexander with relative ease, for he ruled an empire with more than two centuries of military victories to its credit while Alexander had only a few. Alexander, however, proved to be a brilliant adversary and defeated Darius in 331 BC. With that conquest the Persian Empire came to an end and Alexander emerged as the new emperor.

For the next ten years, he marched across Persia, penetrating into India and conquering all the nations he encountered. In India, exhausted from many battles, his otherwise dedicated army refused to go any further. Alexander reluctantly returned to his capital in Babylon and within a few years died of a fever at the age of thirty-two.

Alexander relished his role as world conqueror. He assumed titles such as god, pharaoh, king, and emperor, and lived in lavish splendor. His army was dedicated to him, carrying out his orders with great devotion.

Though Alexander is recognized as a military genius, his greatest impact was the social and historical legacy he left. During his reign, the intertestamental era began, as did the transition from "ancient" to "modern" history. He also brought European and Near Eastern cultures in much closer contact than ever before and spread Hellenism throughout his conquered lands. (Hellenism is a term derived from "Hellas," the ancient name for Greece, and denotes the introduction of Greek culture as the dominant social movement of the era.)

As a young man Alexander gained a profound appreciation for Greek culture from his teacher Aristotle. In his adult role as leader of the Hellenic League, he was able to plant that culture throughout his empire. As an example of the esteem in which he held Greek culture, he founded seventy cities throughout his empire, most named Alexandria or Alexandretta, with each one patterned after a Greek city-state. The most famous of those cities was Alexandria, Egypt, whose beauty was said to rival or surpass that of Athens.

Alexander pursued his Hellenizing policy for two reasons. One was because he believed that fourth century BC Greek culture represented the highest achievement of the human spirit and he wanted all people to have its benefits. The other reason was that he believed that a unified culture was necessary to govern his vast empire. By having a common language, currency, religion, and artistic base, it would be possible to rule effectively. Virtually all subject nations embraced Hellenism in their lands.

This policy had a profound effect on the Jews in the three centuries which followed—especially that part of the policy which affected their religion. For the majority of the pagan nations, worshiping the Greek gods was a simple matter, for they only had to add them to the gods they already had. For the Jews this was prohibited, as they believed that there was only one true God and he alone was to be worshiped.

It is not clear whether Alexander understood the religious implications of his policy as it affected the Jews. It had, however, disastrous consequences for them over the years. Thousands of them died in tumultuous battles because they refused to worship the Greek gods.

To further complicate matters, some Jews embraced Hellenism, including some of their religious leaders and those of the upper class. This pitted not only Jew against gentile, but Jew against Jew.

For the next three hundred years Hellenism played a significant and sometimes tragic role in Jewish life. Many of the messianic hopes, apocalyptic writings, and the rise of rebel groups may be traced in part to the yearning some Jews had to be free of Hellenistic influence—an influence they believed perverted their faith.

The Ptolemies
(323 BC — 30 BC)

Key People:

> **Ptolemy I Lagos**, Macedonian general who received one-fourth of Alexander the Great's empire following his death
>
> **Seleucus I Nicator**, Macedonian general who received one-fourth of Alexander the Great's empire following his death

Key Dates:

323 BC	death of Alexander the Great and division of his empire between four top generals
323 BC	rule of Egypt and Palestine by the Ptolemies
198 BC	defeat of Ptolemies by Seleucids, who then ruled Palestine
30 BC	end of rule of Egypt by the Ptolemies following defeat by Rome

Summary:

Following the unexpected death of Alexander the Great, a power struggle developed for control of his kingdom. Four of his top generals emerged as leaders and Alexander's kingdom was divided among them. Two of them were Ptolemy I Lagos, who received Egypt and Palestine, and Seleucus I Nicator, who received Syria and Babylonia. The other two generals do not figure in biblical history. The Ptolemies transformed Egypt into a Greek society, following the example of Alexander the Great. The Jews were not forced to accept this Greek culture (Hellenism), though many did. The Jews in Jerusalem continued their traditional Jewish life. After about a century of Ptolemaic rule, the Seleucids captured Palestine, a land they long wanted. The Jews began a long period of conflict in which the Seleucids finally demanded that the Jews accept all aspects of Hellenism, including that of Greek polytheistic religion.

Following the untimely death of Alexander the Great, a power struggle developed for the control of the empire. He undoubtedly assumed he would have a long career as ruler and therefore made no provision for a successor. At the time of his death he had an unborn son and a mentally incompetent half-brother. That situation set the stage for serious competition for his throne.

For several years various men vied for it and in time two of his top generals, Ptolemy I Lagos and Seleucus I Nicator, emerged as leading contenders. Because neither one was able to gain supremacy over the other, the southern part of Alexander's kingdom was divided between them. Ptolemy gained Egypt and Palestine while Seleucus gained Syria and Babylonia. The Ptolemies ruled Palestine until 198 BC when the Syrians, who long wanted it, finally conquered the land after years of conflict.

The Ptolemies continued their rule of Egypt until 30 BC when the Romans captured it.

An important feature that characterized the rule of both the Ptolemies and the Seleucids was their commitment to Alexander's goal of Hellenizing all the lands they ruled. This meant that these two rulers and their descendants enforced with varying degrees of intensity that goal and the world they governed was socialized by that culture.

Egypt, the land which the Ptolemies ruled, was known for three thousand years for its distinctive pharaonic culture. That culture is preserved for us today in museums and pictures which depict life under the pharaohs. The Ptolemies transformed Egypt into a Greek culture, a transformation which had profound effects. Greek architecture, language, dress, and other aspects of Hellenism dominated the nation, at least in the great cities.

The Ptolemies not only introduced Hellenism into Egypt but also a new way of governing the land. The pharaohs who previously ruled had a religious component to their governance in that they were seen as gods or offsprings of gods. All aspects of the government were influenced by this perception. The Ptolemies, on the other hand, approached governing much as a business. Their taxation policy, for example, was such that many land owners were forced into life-long indebtedness to the Ptolemies, a practice not very common under the pharaohs.

The historian Philo reports that about one million Jews lived in Egypt. They came in greatest number during four different periods. The first was in 721 BC when Assyria conquered Israel. To escape the forced migration to Assyrian lands thousands of Jews fled to Egypt, settling in large numbers in Alexandria in the north, and Elephantine, an island in the Nile River not far from the present Aswan Dam in southern Egypt. Others came over the course of several years because greater financial opportunity was available in Egypt than in their homeland. The third great wave of people came in 586 BC when Babylon captured Jerusalem. Thousands of Jews were taken into exile in Babylon while other thousands fled to Egypt to escape that captivity. The last wave came in 323 BC when the Ptolemies gained Palestine and in so doing captured thousands of men and forced them into armed service.

Almost four hundred years passed from the time of the first great Jewish migration until the rule of the Ptolemies. During that time, the Jews established themselves firmly in Egypt. As in other places in which they lived, they raised their families, had businesses, and served in leadership roles.

As the years went on, the influence of Hellenism began to make deep inroads into the life of the Jews. It is to the credit of the Ptolemies that they did not force the Jews to accept the religious aspects of Hellenism in Egypt or in Palestine, which they also governed. Yet in subtle ways it began to change the Jews.

Because the Greek language was the primary language used in daily affairs, the Jews eventually lost much of their familiarity with the Hebrew language. Hebrew had been replaced by Aramaic during the Babylonian and Persian periods. Now Greek was replacing Aramaic as the language of daily use. As Greek became the language of common use, there was a danger that many Jews would lose knowledge of their scripture and consequently of the daily practices required by their faith. To remedy the matter the first-ever full translation of the Hebrew Bible was made into Greek. This translation is called the Septuagint version of the Bible, a Greek word meaning "seventy," for legend has it that seventy translators prepared it. That translation was a giant step in helping the Greek-speaking Jews retain their understanding of the requirements of their religion. It was used by Greek-speaking Jews and later also by Christians for several centuries. In another section the account which surrounds that version of the Bible will be presented in greater detail.

In the earlier section on the Persian Empire it was mentioned that following the Babylonian exile the Jews settled in large numbers in four areas of the world: Jerusalem, Babylonia,

Egypt and other lands. In each of those areas the Jews developed their religion and daily life according to the region in which they lived. The Jews who lived on the island of Elephantine in the Nile River, for example, even built a temple similar to the one in Jerusalem. There they conducted worship which at times was at variance with what the Jerusalem leaders believed was proper. In time, the Egyptian priests destroyed that temple. It is not known if it was ever rebuilt.

Though those differences caused antagonism among various Jewish groups, there were three issues which were common offenses for them: Hellenism (the imposition of Greek culture and religion), foreign oppression (the fact that they as God's people were governed by pagans), and taxes (the payment of monies to support their conqueror's armies and religions). Those three issues plagued the Jews, often with violent consequences, for at least three centuries.

The rule of the Ptolemies over Palestine came to an end in 199 BC when, after numerous battles, the Seleucids of Syria finally conquered it. It was during the Seleucid rule, when Antiochus IV was king, that the Jews faced their most difficult period regarding the impact of Hellenism. For, as we shall see, Antiochus required, sometimes to the point of death, that the Jews observe the worship of foreign gods. This set the stage for a new era of rebellion and tragic conflict.

The Seleucids
(199 BC — 167 BC)

Key People:

> **The Seleucids,** rulers of Palestine, Syria and Babylon
>
> **Antiochus III the Great,** Syrian (Seleucid) ruler who captured Palestine from the Egyptians (Ptolemies)
>
> **Hannibal,** general from Carthage in northern Africa who sought to aid Antiochus the Great in his attack on Rome
>
> **Seleucus IV,** son of Antiochus III who ruled the Seleucid Empire
>
> **Antiochus IV Epiphanes** ("god manifest") who severely persecuted the Jews
>
> **Sadducees,** the priestly ruling class in Jerusalem who favored Hellenism
>
> **Pharisees,** laity who were expert in Jewish law and who opposed Hellenism

Key Dates:

> 198 BC   conquest of Egypt, which surrendered Palestine to Syria
>
> 167 BC   major attack against Antiochus IV Epiphanes by Jewish rebels

Summary:

The Seleucids long wanted Palestine for three reasons. They valued it for its rich timber and mineral resources, its role as a buffer state between them and Egypt as long as they did not possess it, and as a staging area in their hope of eventually conquering Egypt. Antiochus the Great finally captured it in 198 BC. Though he advocated Hellenism, he did not force its religious aspects on the Jews until his defeat by the Romans. Following that defeat the Romans demanded exorbitant taxes from the Syrians who in turn extracted high taxes from the Jews. A later leader, Antiochus IV

Epiphanes, issued an edict banning the Jewish religion and forcing, to the point of death, obedience to his edict and the embracing of Greek religion by the Jews. This edict set the stage for the overthrow of the Seleucids by a rebel Jewish family and the beginning of the Maccabean era.

Following the death of Alexander the Great in 323 BC, his empire was divided between four of his top generals with Seleucus I Nicator gaining control of Syria and Babylonia. For the next century the Seleucids fought the Ptolemies of Egypt for control of Palestine for three reasons: one was because Palestine adjoined Syria and was a natural buffer against any possible Egyptian invasion. The second reason was because Palestine served as a vital trade route and was rich in timber and minerals. Lastly, the Seleucids wanted to conquer Egypt, and Palestine was the prime staging area for that conquest.

The Seleucids governed their lands along Hellenistic lines, for they were committed to implementing the policy Alexander the Great initiated when he ruled those territories. Our knowledge of this period of Jewish history comes from the writings of the Jewish historian Josephus and from the apocryphal books of I and II Maccabees. From those references we gain a picture of the suffering and loss the Jews endured, especially under its later Syrian rulers. The following is a review of the events of the period of Syrian rule over Palestine from the time Syria wrested it from Egypt in 198 BC until the Maccabees overthrew them in 176 BC.

The leader who defeated the Egyptians and thereby gained Palestine was King Antiochus III the Great (so named because of his ability to unite the Syrian Empire). Initially the Jews received Antiochus well, for he appeared to continue the practice the Egyptians maintained of permitting the Jews to follow their own religion. Although Antiochus and all other Syrian kings were committed to Hellenism, he did not force the religious aspect of it on the Jews.

In time, Antiochus became alarmed over the growing power of the Roman armies which were conquering nearby nations. He believed that if he attacked them before they became too powerful he could stop their advance. He enlisted the support of Hannibal, the famed Carthaginian general from northern Africa, and attacked the Roman forces. He seriously misjudged their strength and was soundly defeated. With that defeat Antiochus also lost his dream of world conquest, for the Romans took away much of his lands and made him ruler over a smaller territory which included Palestine. Because of his insolence in attacking, the Romans imposed heavy taxes on him—a condition which caused many problems for years to come. Antiochus was required to raise those monies and that changed his relationship with the Jews, as he placed them under heavy financial burdens.

To pay Roman taxes, Antiochus taxed all the peoples he governed and when the tax revenue was not sufficient, he plundered both the Jewish and pagan temples of their wealth. (Ancient temples often served the function which banks do today of being a place where citizens placed their money for safe keeping, since the temples were sacred precincts). Plundering the sacred temple of the Jews was a great offense because that money was consecrated to the service of God, not the maintenance of idolatrous governments and their armies. The Jews rebelled at this practice and many lost their lives in their struggles with the king. It was during a robbery of a pagan temple that Antiochus was murdered, and his son Seleucus IV became king.

Seleucus ruled for twelve years and during those years he found himself in the same situation as that of his father: paying the Romans by extracting high taxes and robbing temples. He, too, was murdered and his son, Antiochus IV Epiphanes ("god manifest") became king.

It was during the reign of Antiochus IV Epiphanes that the Jews came under severe persecution. From his point of view two primary factors guided his rule: the need to pay Rome its taxes and the need to impose Hellenism as the means by which his empire would be united.

The Jews were divided regarding Antiochus. Some, notably the upper class (which included some of the priestly Sadducees), favored his Hellenizing policy. They personally gained position, power, and wealth by siding with Antiochus and were reluctant to surrender those privileges. The Sadducees believed that it was necessary to support him, for then they were free to conduct the temple's affairs. The common people, conservative Jews, and the Pharisees opposed that policy and inevitable conflicts developed among the different groups.

This Hellenizing policy was perhaps one of the reasons many of the opposition groups formed, such as the Pharisees, Zealots, Essenes and other resistance groups. It was also the occasion for the rise of messianic expectations and the writing of apocalyptic literature. These topics will be elaborated upon in a later section, but for now it can be mentioned that the stricter Jews viewed their task as countering the religious implications of Hellenism and foreign oppression.

Antiochus reigned for fifteen years. During that period, opposition to his rule increased. One example showing the reasons the Jews opposed him can be seen in the way he handled the office of high priest. The Jews believed that it came by divine appointment through family lineage. Antiochus placed men in that office through force, and bribery by the highest bidder. On one occasion when the Jews deposed a man he placed in office, Antiochus retaliated by killing hundreds of Jews. Acts such as these only served to increase their hatred of him.

The city of Jerusalem was in a state of constant upheaval during Antiochus's reign, with brutal battles frequently occurring. The conflict between him and the Jews came to a head when he issued a decree forbidding the exercise of the Jewish religion — a decree he enforced through threat of death. He hoped in this way to stop persistent Jewish challenges to his authority and get on with his plan of unifying his empire by Hellenism.

His hope quickly died as his decree set the stage for the Maccabean revolt and a hundred year era of Jewish struggles for independence. That independence was costly, as many lost their lives in battle; and it did not fully rid the Jews of Syrian influence. The Maccabean era, however, set the stage for a period of religious freedom and for a greater role in inter- national politics than at any other time in ancient history.

The Maccabees
(167 BC — 134 BC)

Key People:
> **Antiochus IV Epiphanes**, Syrian king whose edict banning
> the Jewish religion caused deep hatred among the Jews
> **Mattathias Hasmon**, Jewish priest from Modein whose
> killing of a Syrian official sparked the Maccabean revolt
> **The Maccabees**, a nickname (which means "hammer") used
> for Mattathias Hasmon and his five sons, John, Simon,
> Judas, Eleazar, and Jonathan

Key Dates:

167 BC	Mattathias Hasmon killed Syrian official and ignited the Maccabean rebellion
164 BC	temple rededicated after defilement by Syrian king — this is celebrated by the festival called Hanukkah ("dedication")
134 BC	death of Simon, the last of the Maccabees

Summary:
> Antiochus IV Epiphanes banned the Jewish religion and all practices at the temple in Jerusalem and ordered all Jews to worship Greek gods. A Jewish man began to observe this edict on order of a Syrian official. Mattathias Hasmon, a Jewish priest, killed both the Jewish worshiper and the Syrian official, igniting the Maccabean revolt against

the Syrians. Mattathias and his five sons were nicknamed "the Maccabees," a word believed to mean "hammer," perhaps because of the quick hammer-like blows he leveled against the Syrian forces. The sons managed to defeat the Syrians and liberate Jerusalem for the first time since Babylon had defeated them in 587/86 BC. The high spiritual purposes of the Maccabees raised strong hopes among the Jews that the messianic era was dawning and that Jerusalem would be ruled by God.

The Maccabean era may be the best known period of the intertestamental years, being the time when that famous family defeated the hated Syrian king, Antiochus IV Epiphanes, and helped give the Jews a century of freedom. Their victory is celebrated today in the Jewish festival of Hanukkah.

Antiochus ruled the Seleucid Empire, which included Palestine; but because the Romans defeated the Seleucids at the battle of Magnesia in 190 BC, his empire became a satellite of Rome. A condition of that relationship was that he had to pay high taxes. Antiochus thus put heavy pressure on the Jews in order to extract those taxes. He also continued his Hellenizing policy; he was determined to have that policy accepted in order that he might govern his domain in a unified manner.

As time went on and some of the Jews resisted his rule, Antiochus's patience wore thin. He accelerated his demands that the Jews accept that policy with all of its religious implications and he did it with actions which profoundly offended them. One incident will illustrate this. He ordered a pig (an animal considered unclean by the Jews) to be slaughtered on the altar in the temple in Jerusalem as a sacrifice to the Greek god Zeus. This act defiled the altar for three years before the Jews were able to reclaim it from the Syrians and cleanse it for use in the worship of God.

As Jewish resistance of his Hellenizing demands continued, Antiochus issued a decree forbidding the practice of the Jewish religion and ordered the practice of the Greek religion. He forbade Sabbath worship, the circumcising of infant boys, the ownership of biblical scrolls, prayers to God and all other religious acts. He then ordered all Jews to sacrifice to Zeus, eat forbidden swine flesh, and many other offensive practices. Failure to obey his decree meant certain punishment and often death.

Profound turmoil developed in Jerusalem as the Jews struggled to stay alive, yet remain faithful to their religion. The precipitating event which touched off the fire storm against Antiochus took place in 167 BC in a little village called Modein, a few miles outside of Jerusalem. The village priest, Mattathias Hasmon, saw a Jew on his way to offer sacrifices to the Lord. A Syrian official stopped him and ordered the man to sacrifice to Zeus instead, an order the man began to follow. Mattathias was enraged and killed both of the men. News of the killing spread quickly throughout the community and an uprising soon followed. Syrian troops and Jewish men led by Mattathias began to battle each other and the famed Maccabean revolt was underway.

Antiochus believed that this revolt would be readily extinguished (as previous ones had been), convinced that he had the majority of the Jews supporting him. That was because he unwisely believed that having the support of the upper class and Sadducees meant that the rest of the Jews would fall in line. To his regret, he seriously misjudged the mood of the larger Jewish population which resented his Hellenizing policy. They joined Mattathias and supported his attack against Antiochus.

Mattathias had five sons named John, Simon, Judas, Eleazar, and Jonathan. This is the family that received the nickname "the Maccabees," a Hebrew word meaning "hammer." This may have been because his son, Judas, devised a guerrilla tactic of fighting the Syrian troops with quick hammer-like blows and then retreating into the many caves around the region until the next occasion for attack.

The rebellion against Antiochus was initially led by Mattathias who had the support of many pious Jews who were determined to preserve their religion. Antiochus saw that those men would not fight on the Sabbath, as their religion forbade it. After a number of them were helplessly killed in this way, Mattathias counseled that God would understand their need to fight on the Sabbath, and with that word the battle was in full swing.

Within three years of the beginning of the revolt, Mattathias died, leaving the leadership of the struggle to Judas, the one for whom the nickname "Maccabee" originated. The accomplishment for which he is best known is that of driving the Syrians out of the temple, cleansing the altar, and rededicating it to God. The ceremony which marks the day of that accomplishment in 164 BC is called Hanukkah, a word meaning "dedication" (of the temple).

Judas knew that regaining the temple was not the end of the struggle against the Syrians; regaining the land and nation for God was the ultimate goal. The pious Jews who initially supported him were content with the temple gain, however. Judas, therefore, turned to others to complete his larger goals; but his plans were cut short when he died in battle.

His brother, Jonathan, succeeded him as leader. Jonathan's chief accomplishment was having the high Syrian taxes abolished. He, too, died in battle in 143 BC. That left Simon, the last living son, to take up the struggle. He proved to be an able military leader and accomplished the feat of driving the Syrians out of Jerusalem. With that accomplishment, the Jews gained religious and political freedom for the first time since Israel fell to the Assyrians in 722/21 BC. One can only guess at the great rejoicing this caused.

Though the Jews were free, they were still under threat of continued Syrian attacks, since the latter governed other parts of Palestine. This freedom, however, was the source of renewed messianic hopes and the belief that God would come to rule the world from Mt. Zion. For several years that hope was nurtured and grew in intensity as the Jews interpreted the signs of the times in messianic terms. Their hopes were dashed a century later as their leaders became increasingly worldly and ultimately lost control of Palestine to the Roman armies.

The hope-filled years of the Maccabean era came to an end with the death of Simon in 134 BC. The thirty-three years of the Maccabees' rule were years of great sacrifices and accomplishments. Before Simon died he chose his son, John Hyrcanus I, to help him govern Palestine. That selection brought the grandsons of Mattathias Hasmon into the forefront as the next era of Jewish leaders.

The Hasmoneans
(134 BC — 63 BC)

Key People:

> **Hasmoneans**, the descendants of the original Maccabees who governed Jerusalem
>
> **John Hyrcanus I**, the first of the Hasmoneans
>
> **Aristobulus I**, son of Hyrcanus who ruled Jerusalem for one year
>
> **Salome Alexandra**, wife of Aristobulus I, who succeeded him as ruler and later ruled Jerusalem following the death of Alexander Janneus, her second husband
>
> **Alexander Janneus**, second husband of Salome Alexandra, who ruled twenty-seven years
>
> **Hyrcanus II**, son of Salome Alexandra who sought control of Jerusalem
>
> **Aristobulus II**, son of Salome Alexandra and brother of Hyrcanus II, who also fought for control of the Jerusalem throne

Key Dates:

> 134 BC   beginning of Hasmonean rule of Palestine
>
> 63 BC   entrance of the Roman army and Rome's control of Palestine

Summary:

> After Simon, the last of the Maccabees, died his son and later descendants ruled Jerusalem. They took for themselves the original family name, Hasmon. The Hasmoneans built Palestine up in geographical and material ways, but lost the spiritual concern which guided the Maccabees. Intrigue, murders, battles, and conflicts were common during the reign of the Hasmoneans. Disillusionment set in for the Jews as messianic hopes faded. The conflict among family members for control of Palestine brought the Romans into the political picture and led to their conquest of the land. Conflicts over political power and Hellenism marked the seventy-one years of Hasmonean rule. The Jewish hope for freedom from foreign rule was dashed as the Romans became their masters.

The reader will recall from the previous section that Mattathias Hasmon and his five sons bore the nickname, "Maccabees," a word meaning "hammer." The grandsons and descendants who followed as rulers of Jerusalem took the original family name and became known as the Hasmoneans. Under their leadership the Jews lost their freedom and gained a new master — Rome.

The Hasmoneans came into power in 134 BC when Simon, the last of the Maccabees, needed assistance governing Jerusalem. He appointed his son, John Hyrcanus I, as governor and military leader. Shortly thereafter, Simon and his two other sons were murdered by the Syrians. With Simon's death, the last of the original Maccabees passed from the scene. John Hyrcanus took up the mantle of leadership. For the next seventy years the Hasmonean dynasty ruled over Palestine until it was succeeded by the Herods.

The Maccabean revolt was ignited by the high spiritual purposes of acquiring religious and political freedom for the Jews in order that the purposes of God would be more fully realized among their people. When the Hasmoneans assumed power those high purposes gradually faded until the period ended in chaos, battles, wickedness, and ultimately, loss of independence.

When John Hyrcanus I assumed control of Jerusalem, he was granted the title of civil leader and high priest. Because he was not of the Davidic line he could not rightfully assume the title of king, though he acted in that capacity.

John Hyrcanus I had several notable achievements during his reign. He promoted the educational, cultural, and artistic endeavors of Jerusalem and generally raised the standard of living for many. One of the complaints against him was that he was more concerned with those earthly achievements than with promoting the spiritual aspects of Jewish life.

He also engaged in numerous battles which brought about considerable territorial expansion during his rule. One area he annexed was Idumea, south of Judah. As will be discussed in a later section, the Herods, who had important roles in Jewish and Roman political life, came from that region.

Hyrcanus is also known as the ruler who destroyed the temple the Samaritans had built on Mount Gerizim — a temple meant to rival the one in Jerusalem. It was never rebuilt, though the Samaritans continue even to the present to worship God on that mountain.

Initially, Hyrcanus favored the Pharisees. He then changed his allegiance to the Sadducees, for he was growing in his acceptance of Hellenism (which the Sadducees also favored). He even changed the Hebrew names of his sons to Greek ones, an act which further antagonized the Pharisees. Hyrcanus began the long slide to worldliness which succeeding rulers followed, much to Judaea's loss.

When Hyrcanus died in 105 BC he intended that his wife succeed him as ruler of Jerusalem. But his son, Aristobulus I, let her starve to death in prison. Aristobulus then killed one of his brothers, imprisoned two others, and took the throne and office of high priest. All of his scheming was in vain, for within a year he died and his wife, Salome Alexandra, became ruler. His one notable achievement was conquering the territory of Galilee and forcing all inhabitants to embrace the Jewish faith, much as his father earlier did with Idumea.

Salome Alexandra was of a more humane bent than her late husband. She freed the two brothers he imprisoned and married one of them, Alexander Janneus. She then decreed that he was the new ruler and high priest.

Janneus's twenty-seven year reign was marked by material prosperity, territorial expansion, and much social turbulence. He continued the Hasmonean tradition of seeking material gain and political power at the expense of the spiritual purposes of the Jews. He sided with the Sadducees against the Pharisees on numerous issues, especially regarding Hellenism, which the Pharisees particularly resented.

An incident of which the historian Josephus wrote surrounds Alexander's misuse of his privilege as high priest. At a festival (probably the Feast of Booths) Alexander stood upon an altar and was going to sacrifice when the populace threw fruits which were used at the festival at him and reviled him for his low birth. He retaliated by killing six thousand of them (*Antiquities* 13.13.5). Because the Sadducees did not intervene and attempt to stop the carnage, the Pharisees held it against them, thus adding to the deepening division between the two groups. Events such as this show the decay which had eaten away the spiritual leadership of the Jews. It was a tragic time.

Following Janneus's death, his wife, Alexandra, resumed control of the throne which she had earlier relinquished to her husband. She ruled for seven relatively calm years. She learned from her husband's experience not to antagonize the Pharisees and in fact gave them considerable control over the day-to-day affairs of administering Jerusalem. However, she held on to the power of administering the larger political decisions which involved other nations.

Alexandra planned to have her older son, Hyrcanus II, succeed to the throne following her death. It came earlier than anticipated and her younger son, Aristobulus II, also set his eyes on the throne. Hyrcanus II was weak compared to his brother who had the fiery temperament of his father Janneus. Aristobulus II raised a large army and proceeded to make plans to take the throne. That set the stage for a series of conflicts which brought Rome into the picture and eventually led to the conquest of Jerusalem by Rome. Because the story of the final struggle between these two brothers for the throne is intimately tied up with the story of Rome's entrance into the scene, the ending of the brothers' story will be reserved for the following two sections.

At this point it can be said that the manner by which the two brothers sought to resolve their differences created much of the setting against which the New Testament story unfolded: the conquest of Jerusalem by the Romans and their placement of the Herods as the rulers over the Jews. With the defeat of those two brothers the Hasmonean dynasty was all but over, and with their deaths came the end of Jewish rule of Palestine for the next two thousand years.

The Romans
(63 BC — 135 AD)

Key People:
> **Pompey**, Roman general who captured Jerusalem
> **Caesar Augustus** (Octavian), first ruler of the Roman
> Empire

Key Dates:

63 BC	Rome conquered Jerusalem and made it subject to the Roman Republic
27 BC	the Roman Empire was born
70 AD	the Romans destroyed the temple in Jerusalem
135 AD	the Romans drove the Jews out of Jerusalem and destroyed it

Summary:

The New Testament period and the last century of the intertestamental era were both played out against the background of the Roman Empire. From its earliest days until the first century BC, Rome had gone through three political stages before it became an empire in 27 BC. A serious conflict between two of the last Hasmonean brothers who vied for control of Jerusalem brought Rome into Jewish politics. Their entrance resulted in the downfall of a free Jerusalem and its subjugation to Rome, which placed Herod and his family on the throne in Jerusalem—an act which caused profound resentment among Jews. That resentment spawned several militant Jewish resistance groups which eventually caused the downfall of Jerusalem.

The story of the end of Hasmonean rule in Palestine is tied up with the Roman conquest of the land and their placement of Herod on the throne in Jerusalem. Therefore, to close the story on the Hasmoneans, the key developments in the history of Rome will first be traced.

The drama of the years immediately preceding the birth of Jesus and the beginning of the Christian church was played out against the background of the vast and powerful Roman Empire. There were four phases in Roman history from the time of its beginning until the time of Jesus. Those stages were: small villages, the monarchy, the republic, and finally, the empire.

Archaeological evidence shows that about two thousand years before the birth of Jesus, groups of people migrated from Europe and Asia and settled in the land now called Italy. There their villages were governed by simple communal governments until the city of Rome was founded in 753 BC.

Legend has it that the city was begun by twin brothers, Romulus and Remus. They were abandoned by their parents, an earthly mother and a father who was the son of the god Mars. A she-wolf found the boys and nursed them, saving their lives. As an adult, Romulus (hence "Rome") marked off the boundaries of the city and became its first king. This is considered the beginning of the monarchy in Italy. It lasted until 509 BC.

The third stage in Rome's development was the republic, which lasted until 27 BC. During this time, it was governed by groups of strong leaders called "senators." Under their leadership Rome made some of its greatest territorial and political advances. At first, it was not the only power of the Mediterranean world (the reader will remember that Alexander the Great was also making significant advances in nearby nations). When the Romans did become the sole power, however, they ruled all territories, including those of Alexander's, with Egypt and Palestine being among the last lands conquered before the New Testament period began.

As the republic grew in strength, it faced its greatest challenge which, if not met successfully, could have meant its end. That challenge was presented by Hannibal and other generals of the Carthaginian armies of northern Africa. From 264 BC until 146 BC the Romans fought them in three separate wars, called the Punic Wars, ultimately defeating them and becoming the dominant world power.

As Roman generals gained spectacular victories, they began to usurp the powers of the senators in governing the republic. The senators had become corrupt, lazy, and self-serving and were no match for the tough and disciplined generals. The conflicts between these two groups came to a head as it became too difficult to govern the sprawling republic in the old ways.

Two opposing views of how to resolve the matter developed. One group, led by Cicero, wanted to keep the republican form of government, but correct the injustices and corruption of the senators. Another group, led by Julius Caesar, wanted to end that form of government and replace it with a strong dictator. From that struggle developed the idea of a triumvirate (a three person regency). It was formed in 60 BC, composed of Julius Caesar, the general Pompey, and Crassus, a rich businessman.

This triumvirate existed about twenty years, with conflicts frequently marking its rule. Then Caesar was murdered and a new triumvirate was formed, composed of Mark Antony, Lepidus, and Octavian (later called Caesar Augustus, see Luke 2:1). It became evident that a triumvirate could not govern the increasingly large empire, and in the ensuing power struggle Octavian emerged as the sole ruler. With his rule the Roman Empire was born in 27 BC.

Octavian/Augustus laid the groundwork for many notable administrative achievements which were continued by his successors for at least two hundred years. These included tax laws, military organization, a vast network of roads linking the empire, social order, and a policy termed the "Pax Romana." This term means the "Roman Peace" and was a militarily enforced keeping of law and order. Disruption of the peace was considered to be a cardinal violation and was severely punished by Augustus's armies.

Rome entered the Jewish political scene when the last two Hasmonean brothers vied for control of the throne. At that time Palestine was loosely under Roman control (through the Syrians who governed it for them). The two brothers, Hyrcanus II and Aristobulus II, fought for control of Jerusalem and appealed to Rome, each hoping Rome would support him.

Rome learned that there was unrest in Jerusalem and that lives had been lost in various conflicts. This unrest was not tolerated by the Romans for whom the "Pax Romana" was a primary political policy. The emperor sent Pompey, a general who was nearby, to settle the matter. It was not, however, easily resolved, for each brother had strong allies who wanted to control Jerusalem. A fierce battle erupted in 63 BC in which Pompey defeated the Jewish forces and claimed Jerusalem for Rome. Rome placed Herod the Great on the Jewish throne to govern on its behalf. The end of the Hasmoneans and the demise of Jewish independence had arrived. For more than a century the Herodian family ruled Palestine, or parts of it, and their influence is keenly felt throughout the New Testament story.

Relations between conservative Jews and the Romans were often troubled and clashes frequently broke out. In one series of conflicts in 70 AD, the Romans partially destroyed Jerusalem and completely destroyed the temple. Jesus foretold that destruction (see Matt 24:1-2). The conflicts between the Jews and the Romans continued for several more years until the last bloody battle took place in 135 AD. During that encounter Jerusalem was completely destroyed and the Jews were banished from the city. They would not regain the city or Palestine as their own for almost two thousand years.

The role of the Herods will be surveyed in the next section, but for now it can be said that with their arrival the intertestamental era came to a close and the New Testament era was born. Those closing years would see an explosion of messianic and apocalyptic hopes as the Jews fought to free themselves of foreign governments and to establish a theocracy.

The Herodians
(37 BC — 94 AD)

Key People:

> **John Hyrcanus I**, Hasmonean ruler who, in 126 BC, ordered all Idumeans to convert to Judaism
>
> **Antipater I**, an Idumean appointed by Hyrcanus II to govern Idumea — Antipater's son also bore the same name, and was the father of Herod the Great
>
> **Hyrcanus II & Aristobulus II**, last of the Hasmonean brothers who contended for the throne in Jerusalem
>
> **Herod the Great**, an Idumean enthroned in Jerusalem by the Romans
>
> **Herodian family**, five descendants of Herod the Great who governed some part of Palestine during the New Testament era

Key Dates:

63 BC	Antipater I became involved in Jewish and Roman political affairs
63 BC	Rome captured Jerusalem
37 BC	Herod the Great appointed king of the Jews by the Romans
4 BC	Herod the Great's death

Summary:

Herod the Great's grandfather and father both played roles in Jewish and Roman political life. Herod managed to win the favor of the Romans and was installed by them as king of the Jews. This greatly troubled the Jews, for he was an Idumean and the Jews believed that only a descendant of King David could occupy the throne. Herod's rule led to many conflicts between him, the Romans, and the Jews. He greatly favored the Hellenizing emphasis of the time and built many Greco-Roman styled buildings in its honor. He sought to appease the Jews by expanding their temple with elaborate additions to it. Herod's slowly developing insanity caused many tragic deaths during his reign.

The Herods first appeared in Jewish political life in 126 BC when John Hyrcanus I, the first Hasmonean king, ruled Palestine. He conquered Idumea (ancient Edom), the land south of Judaea, and decreed that all of its inhabitants were required to convert to Judaism. This brought thousands of mixed blood Jews, Arabs, and Gentiles into the Jewish fold. He then appointed an Idumean, Antipater I, as its governor. (This was Herod the Great's grandfather.)

Some years later, in 63 BC, Antipater's son, Antipater II, became involved in the disintegrating affairs of the Hasmonean rulers of Palestine. Their rule lasted only twenty five more years before it collapsed in defeat under Roman might.

The younger Antipater saw the power struggle that was taking place between the two brothers, Hyrcanus II and Aristobulus II, for Palestine's throne. This was no mere struggle between two brothers, for each had sizable factions of the populace supporting him with substantial armies ready to fight. The Pharisees and the common people supported Hyrcanus II and his anti-Hellenizing policy. The Sadducees and the well-to-do supported Aristobulus II and his pro-Hellenizing policy. The city of Jerusalem was deeply divided on the issue.

Antipater II went to Hyrcanus II and said that he would support him in his effort to capture the throne. Hyrcanus agreed to accept his support and, in the battle which followed, he defeated his brother. The victory was short-lived, however, for Aristobulus II gained new support and again attacked his brother.

To resolve the matter, both brothers appealed to Rome for help. Rome did not respond immediately; and this angered Aristobulus, who took it on himself to attack Jerusalem once again. This attack angered the Romans, who ordered Pompey, a general who was nearby, to go to Jerusalem and settle the matter. A major battle was waged in the city and twelve thousand of Aristobulus's troops and defenders were slain. This battle brought the city of Jerusalem under direct Roman control in 63 BC. Two serious consequences followed: Hasmonean rule came to an end, as did the Jews' century-long independence.

During all this chaos, Antipater was busy gaining the trust of the Romans. He managed to persuade them that he was on their side and helped them in their struggle against the Hasmonean brothers. They rewarded him by permitting him to name his two sons to important political posts in Palestine. He appointed his son Phasael as military governor of Judaea and Herod, his other son, as military governor of Galilee. Roman intrigues were ever present. Antipater fell victim to them and was poisoned. His son Phasael then committed suicide. This left Herod to contend with the Romans alone. He proved himself to be an able administrator and ally of the Romans who rewarded him by making him king of the Jews in 37 BC. The Jews deeply resented this appointment, for they believed that only a descendant of David should occupy the throne in Jerusalem; and Herod was a mixed blood Idumean, considered unworthy to rule God's people.

Herod the Great proved to be a many-sided ruler, much valued by the Romans and despised by the Jews. There were three primary reasons the Jews hated him:

The first reason was that he was not a true Jew. His Idumean background made him a mixed blood person and for such to occupy David's throne was a great offense to many Jews. He was also seen as a puppet of the Romans, and he employed spies, threats, and murders to maintain his throne.

Second, he was strongly committed to promoting Hellenism in Palestine — a policy the Romans also wanted enforced. Herod went on a building spree, erecting castles, temples, gymnasiums, parks, fortresses, and libraries — all in Greco-Roman style, celebrating the Greco-Roman spirit. To appease the Jews he elaborately rebuilt their temple, a task which took more than eighty years to complete. It's glory was short-lived, however, for as Jesus prophesied, it was soon to be destroyed. In 70 AD that came to pass (Mark 13:1-2; Matt 24:1-2; Luke 21:5-6).

The third reason the Jews despised him was because of his evil deeds. He murdered his wife, children, friends, and enemies alike. Some believe that this occurred because he began to go insane following the death of his first wife. Herod's evil sister told him that his wife, Mariamne, was having an affair with his best friend. Herod had them both killed only to learn later that his sister had lied to him. Over the years this tragedy, coupled with his own evil bent, caused his insanity to increase as he feared others would take his throne. He killed all who posed that threat — even some of his children.

From 37 BC until 94 AD, Herod or one of his descendants ruled the Jews. Their names are recorded in the New Testament. In order they were: Herod the Great, 37 — 4 BC (Matt 2:1); Herod Archelaus, 4 BC — 6 AD (Matt 2:22); Herod

Antipas, 4 BC—39 AD (Matt 14:3); Herod Philip, 4 BC—34 AD (Luke 3:1); Herod Agrippa I, 37—44 AD (Acts 12:2); and Herod Agrippa II, 50—94 AD (Acts 26:28).

With the reign of Herod the Great, the intertestamental era ended and the New Testament era began. With the last of the Herods, the New Testament era closed. That family played a powerful role in both Jewish and early Christian history as they governed the people on behalf of Rome.

During the reign of Herod the Great, powerful Jewish rebellious forces were at work. The longing to overthrow Herod and the Romans bred apocalyptic and messianic fevers. From a political point of view the rebellions were in vain, for the Romans ultimately destroyed Jerusalem in 135 AD. They drove the Jews out, not to return for two thousand years.

3
RELIGIOUS DEVELOPMENTS
IN THE INTERTESTAMENTAL ERA

Most of the elements which make up the New Testament story had their beginnings, not during the Old Testament period, but during the intertestamental years. In this chapter we will show some of the main literary developments, groups, movements, institutions, and ideas of that time.

Literature and Scripture

Apocalyptic Literature. A new and powerful form of religious literature developed among the Jews during the intertestamental era and among Christians during the first two centuries of their era. This was apocalyptic literature, a term meaning "to reveal." The book of Daniel, in part, and the book of Revelation are two such works which are included in the Bible. Their purpose was to reveal God's plan for history which included a final world conflict, which would end the power of evil and death, and the establishment of God's eternal and righteous kingdom, where believers would dwell.

Apocalyptic literature grew out of prophetic literature; each was prophesying the future. Prophetic literature did so with words (Isa 50:1), and apocalyptic literature did it with word pictures and symbolism (Rev 1:1).

The hardships and sufferings which the Jews and Christians endured at the hands of their Syrian or Roman overlords gave rise to apocalyptic. Jewish apocalyptic literature began after the return from the Babylonian exile as Palestinian Jews longed for release from the oppression of unbelieving rulers. As their hopes for release increased, so did their oppression and suffering. That led them to believe that they were not fighting human forces alone, but through them, demonic ones also. That meant that a cosmic war pitting divine forces against those demonic ones was the only solution.

To convey the epic nature of that conflict, ordinary combatants would not do. Figures larger than life and of heroic proportions were needed, and thus was born the unique word pictures of the apocalypses. Some Christians shared the same concept of the Jews regarding this cosmic battle, and cast their conviction in the same heroic pictures. The book of Revelation vividly portrays that end-time battle.

Apocalyptic literature is often baffling to today's readers. However, its message was understood by the intended audience of the time, though veiled to the oppressors. The apocalypses' message of God's ultimate completion of his plan to save the world and establish his eternal kingdom gave the believers great hope and encouragement in the face of many hardships and sufferings.

The Apocrypha. The Old Testament Apocrypha is a collection of fifteen Jewish works written in Egypt and Palestine between 200 BC and 100 AD. They range from historical to fictional and inspirational works.

The word *apocrypha* means "hidden." Originally these works were hidden from the average person because it was believed they were too lofty for them. The Protestant reformers later hid (i.e., removed) them from the Bible, for they believed these works contained historical and doctrinal errors. A brief survey of the views of the three main religious bodies regarding these books will be helpful.

The Jewish rabbis did not include the books of the Apocrypha in 90 AD, when they established their list of approved biblical books. Four reasons were behind their decision:

1. Only books decreed by Ezra as authoritative were acceptable.
2. Some of these works contained historical errors.
3. The rabbis disapproved of the early Christians' use of them to show that Jesus was the messiah.
4. Only works written in Hebrew were acceptable, for they believed God delivered the original texts in Hebrew. The apocryphal books were written in Greek and were incorporated into the Septuagint, the Greek translation of the Old Testament.

The Roman Catholic church accepted these works as biblical, even though there was an extensive debate between Jerome and Augustine, two of the church's greatest scholars. Jerome appreciated their spiritual value, but sided with Jewish findings that these works contained some historical errors. Nevertheless, he included translations of them in his Latin Vulgate version of the Bible. Augustine argued that since the texts had been used as scripture by the early Christians for some centuries, they should continue to be accepted. Augustine's view prevailed, and these writings are in the Catholic Old Testament.

From the time of the reformers, Protestants have omitted the writings for two reasons. One is that they agreed with the Jewish scholars that errors exist in the texts. The second reason is that some of the works support doctrines which they rejected. The efficacy of prayers and mass for the dead are cases in point (2 Macc 12:43-45).

Whatever position one accepts regarding these works, they do bear reading because they give important insights into the spirituality of the intertestamental period.

The Septuagint. The creation of the Septuagint version of the Bible, the Old Testament in the Greek language, was one of the great literary creations of the intertestamental era. However, the fact that it was written in a language other than Hebrew caused controversy. Greek speaking Jews hailed it, saying that it made the Bible available to more people, while many Palestinian Jews decried it, as they believed that Hebrew was the divine language and could not be tampered with.

The Septuagint (a Greek word meaning "seventy," thus sometimes also identified by the roman numerals for seventy, LXX) is more properly called a version rather than a translation. That is because, though much of it is a close translation of the standard Hebrew text, in other places it relied upon different Hebrew texts and even includes some portions which were originally written in Greek.

The origin of the Septuagint is not fully known, though it is believed to have been produced in Alexandria, Egypt, around 250 BC. A popular legend, which scholars now discount as inaccurate, was that the head of the great library in Alexandria, Demetrius of Phalerum, requested from the Jewish leaders a copy of their Bible in Greek in order that the Egyptian authorities would better understand the life and religion of the million Jews who lived in Egypt. The elders in Jerusalem complied with the request and sent seventy (or seventy-two) scholars to complete the task, which they did in seventy days (hence the name Septuagint).

Though the origin of the Septuagint is not fully known, its importance is evident. During that period in Jewish life the Hellenizing process was in full progress in Egypt. Greek was the common language, and because of that, many Jews lost the knowledge of Hebrew. If that condition continued, it was evident that in time the Jews would also lose knowledge of their religion. To avoid that possibility, the version was prepared — a step which was to have great significance for future generations of Jews and Christians.

The Septuagint contains the books which Protestants associate with the Old Testament, plus the fifteen books they call the Apocrypha. The diaspora Jews used this version until early in the first century AD, but then largely abandoned it. The early Christians used this version of the Old Testament for several centuries. Since the Reformation, Protestants have not used this version, though Anglican and Orthodox churches accept apocryphal books. In the Roman Catholic community, these books are known as "deutero-canonical."

The Old Testament quotations found in the New Testament are largely drawn from the Septuagint.

The Dead Sea Scrolls. The greatest literary find of the twentieth century came by accident as a young Bedouin shepherd, searching for a lost goat in some caves in an area called Qumran near the Dead Sea, found the Dead Sea scrolls in long-hidden pottery.

The term, "Dead Sea scrolls," originally referred to the 800 manuscripts and thousands of manuscript fragments which were found in eleven caves at Qumran from 1947 to 1956. Later, the term was applied to additional manuscripts discovered elsewhere in the Judean desert. These were not biblically related manuscripts, as are many of the Qumran scrolls, but mostly concerned the ill-fated revolt against the Romans led by Bar-Kochba in 132–135 AD. There are also some family archives and some 7th and 8th century Christian documents.

The Dead Sea scrolls were written in Hebrew, Aramaic, and Greek, and were produced on parchment, papyrus, leather, and copper. Of the 800 manuscripts, 270 are biblical books and the remaining 530 are commentaries, interpretations of the Bible, rules of the community which produced the writings (possibly the Essenes), hymns, and similar religious writings. At least part of every book of the Old Testament (except Esther) has been preserved. The longest document was the book of Isaiah, of which there are several scrolls.

It is thought that the religious community which produced these works did so over a two hundred year period, from the mid second century BC until the destruction of the temple in 70 AD.

These documents are valuable for several reasons. One is that they confirm that our present Old Testament is reasonably faithful to those ancient manuscripts. These scrolls are about

1000 years older than the oldest existing copy of the complete Hebrew Bible, and show that little changed in the copying of the texts over the centuries. The non-biblical documents are a rich source of knowledge of Jewish life and belief during the intertestamental era. They supplement the information provided by writers such as Josephus and Philo, and reveal a dynamic and diverse Jewish life. One also sees from these texts how the Jews used different versions of the Bible, such as the Septuagint and Aramaic targums, in preparing their biblical texts. In short the Dead Sea scrolls greatly enrich our knowledge of the text of the Old Testament and reveal a dynamic Judaism in the intertestamental years.

Major Jewish Groups and Movements

The Samaritans. The Samaritans are included in this study not because they originated during the intertestamental era, but because of special developments in their society which affected that era and the New Testament story.

The Samaritans came into being following Assyria's conquest of Israel in 722/21 BC. The Assyrians deported many Jews to various nations, then transported people from those nations to the land of Israel. Those transported people intermarried with the Jews who remained and thus were born the Samaritans. The exiled Jews rejected these people whom they considered hybrid Jews, for not only were they of mixed blood, but they incorporated elements of Assyrian religion into Judaism. An example of this rejection is seen almost two hundred years later when the Jews who returned from the Babylonian exile refused to permit the Samaritans to help them rebuild the temple and the city of Jerusalem.

In 130 BC the Jewish king, John Hyrcanus, issued a decree that all people who lived in Palestine were to convert to Judaism and follow its teachings. This meant that other religions were forbidden—a decree which deeply affected the Samaritans who differed from the Jews on some key beliefs.

The Samaritans believed that the capital of the holy land was Shechem, the original capital, while the Jews believed it to be Jerusalem. The Samaritans believed that the temple was to be on Mount Gerizim near Samaria, while the Jews believed it was to be in Jerusalem. The Samaritans accepted only the written Torah while the Jews accepted a larger collection of works including the Prophets and the Writings.

Hyrcanus ordered the destruction of the temple in which the Samaritans worshiped—an act that virtually severed any hope of reconciliation between the Samaritans and the Jews. Though small in number, the Samaritans continue outdoor worship of God atop Mount Gerizim to this day. It is against this background of hostility between Jews and Samaritans that Jesus' outreach to the Samaritans had its significance.

The Essenes. A heightened revolutionary mood coupled with messianic expectations pervaded Jewish consciousness from the time of the Maccabees until the destruction of the temple (167 BC to 70 AD). The Essenes contributed to that consciousness with goals of ridding Palestine of foreign rule, cleansing Israel of sin, and helping usher in the messianic age. Information regarding them comes from the historian Josephus, the philosopher Philo, and perhaps the Dead Sea scrolls found in the Qumran caves. (It must be mentioned here that there is considerable debate in progress regarding the relationship of the Dead Sea Scrolls, the Qumran community, and the Essenes. Some argue for a close relationship while others see none at all. Our purpose at this point is only to give a brief glimpse of what is known of the practices of the Essenes.)

The Essenes were at the height of their influence just before the Christian era and numbered a few thousand members. Most of them were celibate men, though a few members were women. They renounced worldly ambition and pleasures, and devoted themselves to holiness and pleasing God. They lived in self-sustaining communities primarily in the desert, although others lived in the cities; some believed that they were guided by the leader who is called the "teacher of righteousness" in some Dead Sea Scrolls.

The Essenes (their name is thought to mean "pious") were Pharisaic in much of their beliefs. Similarities end there, for in many ways they outdid the Pharisees with their intense devotion to the practice of various spiritual disciplines. Two areas were of special concern to them: the Torah and the temple.

Each morning and evening significant amounts of time were given to the study of the Torah, the first five books of the Bible. Every letter of every word was studied because it was believed that God gave each word and none could be overlooked, lest an obligation from God be missed. The Essenes produced many copies of biblical books as well as numerous studies related to the spiritual life. They also scrupulously observed all the feasts, rituals, washings, and sacrifices. They did not go to the temple in Jerusalem, for they believed the temple priesthood to be corrupt. This led them to have their own priests who administered the temple activities for them in their communes.

It is believed that the Essene movement came to an end when it was caught up in the destruction of Jerusalem by the Romans in 70 AD. But their legacy of a pursuit for holiness continues today among Jews and Christians alike.

The Pharisees.   The Pharisees (their name probably means "separated") were members of a lay movement which began about the same time as the priestly Sadducees did around 150 BC, shortly after the Maccabean revolt. They formed for the purpose of separating themselves from sin through strict adherence to the scriptures in order to be holy for God. In the New Testament this movement was portrayed as having certain of its key leaders veer from that high purpose and turn toward a troubling legalism.

The seeds of Pharisaism were sown during the Babylonian exile when the Jews were separated from their temple. Study of the scripture was substituted for temple worship, and when they returned to Jerusalem they continued that study. Laymen who were wise regarding scripture and personally pious in their spiritual lives were accepted as teachers in the newly forming synagogues. These men were called "Hasidim" or "pious ones" and were the forerunners of the Pharisees.

During the Maccabean revolt, the Hasidim were in the forefront of the struggle to defeat the hated Syrian king, Antiochus IV Epiphanes, who sought to ban the Jewish religion. When they successfully overthrew him, the Hasidim retreated from the political struggle against the Syrians. With that withdrawal they faded from the scene and the Pharisees emerged to continue their struggle. Like the Hasidim, the Pharisees pursued their desire to promote holiness in the nation, but they did it with greater intensity and in a more formalized manner.

The Pharisees held secular employment while also becoming experts in the sacred scriptures. St. Paul, who was a Pharisee and a tentmaker, is an example. The Pharisees accepted all written scripture as well as the oral traditions which accompanied it. The Sadducees, on the other hand, believed that all doctrines had to be found in the Torah (first five books) in the written tradition, otherwise doctrines from oral tradition were not acceptable. This caused major conflicts between the two groups. The Pharisees passed from the scene soon after the temple was destroyed in 70 AD and were gradually replaced by the rabbis, who followed Pharisaic practice for the most part.

The Sadducees. Most of what is known about the Sadducees comes from the historian Josephus, the New Testament, and the Mishnaic/Talmudic traditions. Virtually nothing is preserved of their work from their own sources. They began during the Maccabean era, as did the Pharisees. Their name was derived either from Zadok, king Solomon's high priest, or from the word *zaddiq*, meaning "righteous."

The Sadducees played two primary roles in Jewish life. Since most of them were priests, wealthy, and well educated, they administered the temple and served on the Sanhedrin, the Jews' court system. The Pharisees were in frequent conflict with the Sadducees, for they believed that the Sadducees favored the foreign governments which ruled them, either Syrian or Roman, as well as their Hellenizing policies. The Sadducees did in fact favor them, for it was through the good graces of the government that the Sadducees held their high social positions and were permitted to administer the temple.

In addition to favoring the government and supporting their Hellenizing policies, the Sadducees clashed with the Pharisees on other important matters. Their chief source of conflict, however, stemmed from their respective views of scripture. The Pharisees accepted all scripture plus the oral traditions which had grown up around them. The Sadducees accepted the written scripture only, and all doctrines had to be found in the Torah (law). This difference regarding scripture became the basis for much conflict between the two groups. In this respect the Pharisees were the liberal wing of the religious establishment while the Sadducees were the conservative ones.

The Sadducees also tended to be more literal and strict when interpreting scripture and applying it to legal cases. The Pharisees were more liberal and flexible when doing so.

When the Romans destroyed the temple in 70 AD, the Sadducees passed from the scene of history, for their life and work were intimately bound up with the temple and its ministry to the Jews.

The Zealots. It has already been noted that the last two centuries of the intertestamental era and the first century after the birth of Jesus were troubled times for the Jews of Palestine. Their great longing was for liberation from pagan rule and to be ruled by God, whose people they were. Following the Macccabean revolt several liberation groups came into being, each with its own agenda as to how this liberation was possible. Of the known groups none was more radical or violent than the Zealots (note the English cognate, "zeal"). They were known to use intimidation, violence, and murder, not only against the Romans but against their fellow Jews whom they suspected of collaborating with the Romans.

The Zealots played a significant role in leading the Jews into their last fateful attacks against the Romans in 70 AD, and again in 132 AD. (A Zealot is mentioned in Luke 6:15 as being among the first of Jesus' disciples). They continually stirred up the people against the Romans and persuaded large numbers of them that they could actually defeat the superior Roman forces, an effort which proved tragically foolish. They may have believed that if they started the conflict, God would be forced to intervene on their behalf.

But the outcome of the war against the Romans was that thousands of Jews lost their lives, the temple was destroyed, and much of Jerusalem was burned to the ground. In 132 AD, when the final Jewish effort was made against the Romans, the Roman armies destroyed the last remnants of the city and drove the remaining Jews from it, an exile which lasted almost two thousand years.

The end of the Zealot movement came during the famed attack of the Romans at Masada, the mountain-top villa and fortress Herod the Great built for himself. The attack at Masada came two years after the fall of Jerusalem in 70 AD. Flavius Silva, the Roman Governor, came to the fortress and found it difficult to reach, for it was atop a sheer cliff. For several months Silva's troops built a long ramp which enabled them to scale to the top. When Silva reached the top he was greeted by a grizzly sight—960 men, women, and children had committed suicide rather than live under Roman rule. Only two women and five children were found alive. That final act of defiance brought to an end the turbulent history of a group which would rather die than surrender its right to live under God's rule as his people.

The Rabbis. The present-day rabbi is the product of several different strands of Jewish leadership which have been woven together over the centuries. Early glimmerings of the use of the term *rabbi* are seen in the closing days of the intertestamental era and its use is primarily that of respect for a learned person. It was not until the end of the New Testament era that it became a formal religious title. The term *rabbi* is derived from a word meaning "great" and suggests respect for a person of great learning. Tracing the key stages of Jewish leadership which led up to the rabbinical office will help the reader put it in historical perspective.

For much of the Old Testament period, there were four religious leadership offices: priest, prophet, sage, and scribe. The priests administered the temple, the prophets were called by God to preach to the people, the sages taught and composed Israel's wisdom literature, and the scribes served as scripture transcribers and teachers of the law.

During the intertestamental era, the role of teacher, whether called sage, scribe or rabbi, became increasingly important in the newly forming synagogues. The Pharisees, as previously mentioned, evolved after the Maccabean uprising from a group of pious laymen who held secular jobs, but were experts in the oral law. The Sadducees, who came into being about the same time as the Pharisees, were either priests or laymen of the wealthy upper class. The Pharisees and scribes served on the various synedria (plural of sanhedrin, Israel's councils), and were also teachers in the synagogues.

During the New Testament era, most of the above mentioned offices continued and the rabbi (literally, "my teacher") began to come into prominence. Almost all of the New Testament references to the term are applied to Jesus. After Rome destroyed Jerusalem in 70 AD, many of the leadership offices ceased, while that of the rabbi began to grow. The rabbi incorporated elements of many of the now defunct offices and the term *rabbi* became an official religious title. By the second century of the Christian era, the rabbinate became the primary leadership force in Judaism, shaping its life for centuries to come, down to the present.

Major Jewish Institutions and Ideas

The Synagogue. A key Jewish institution which began shortly before the start of the intertestamental era and continues today was the synagogue, a word which means, "place of assembly." It is believed that it began around 550 BC while the Jews were exiled in Babylon.

For the four hundred years prior to the beginning of the synagogue, the temple in Jerusalem was the focus of Jewish religious life. The Bible taught that worship, especially sacrifice, could only be offered on the temple altar. That mandate posed a serious problem for those in Babylon, a thousand miles from Jerusalem. How could the biblical mandate for worship be properly fulfilled in that condition? To answer this question, the Jews turned to some of their greatest spiritual leaders: Isaiah, Jeremiah, and Ezekiel.

Those great spiritual lights taught them that God was not confined to the temple, but could be worshiped anywhere. They also taught that spiritual sacrifice was possible — the sacrifice of prayer with a humble and contrite heart. These insights caused the people to come together in small groups in homes to study the Bible and to pray. From these humble beginnings the synagogue was born.

Initially the groups were self-led. In time certain men who demonstrated superior insight and high moral character were asked to teach the groups. These were laymen who were unpaid and held secular employment to maintain themselves. Over the years some of these teachers gained wide followings and their thoughts, which were commentaries on scripture, were preserved in the writings called the Talmud.

When the Jews returned from Babylon they rebuilt the temple, but continued the development of the synagogue. Eventually the people moved from homes and built buildings for their synagogues. When the Romans destroyed the temple in 70 AD, the synagogues replaced it as the place for Jewish worship and study, eventually spreading world-wide.

The Sanhedrin. An institution which came into being during the intertestamental era and played a significant role in the life of Jesus and the early Christian community was the Sanhedrin, a word meaning "council." Among other decisions which affected the early Christians, the Sanhedrin approved the death of Jesus and St. Paul's imprisonment. For an institution which played so vital a role in early Christianity it is disappointing to know that few records of its workings are preserved in early sources. However, the major source for our knowledge of it comes from the Talmudic tractate, "Sanhedrin."

The Jewish historian Josephus wrote that the Sanhedrin was founded between 150 BC and 125 BC. It was headed by the high priest, who presided over the seventy-member body (a number chosen based on Moses' selection of seventy elders to help him govern the emerging Jewish nation, see Num 11:16). There is evidence also for a little Sanhedrin in Jerusalem composed of twenty-three members. Most leading towns and cities also had a Sanhedrin.

Membership on the "council" was made up primarily of Pharisees, Sadducees, and scribes. The scribes were lawyers who may have been either Pharisees or Sadducees. It is not clear from early sources how a member was chosen for the council, how long the term of office was, or how removal was determined if the need arose.

The primary role of the Sanhedrin was to be supremely versed in the sacred writings and oral traditions which surrounded them, for from these sources the religious, political, and legal decisions of Israel were established. The Great Sanhedrin of Jerusalem was in effect the Supreme Court of the nation of Israel, and held powers most of which pertained to national matters. The Jerusalem synedria (plural of Sanhedrin) met in the temple precincts. Records indicate that there were numerous local courts from which a case that could not be decided there would escalate to the Jerusalem synedria. These smaller courts were established to try specific cases of local concerns.

This system served the Jews for about two hundred years, but was dissolved in 66 AD, four years before the Romans destroyed the temple. Following its dissolution, it was reorganized by a governing body of rabbis, which served the Jews for several more centuries.

Messianic Expectations. The idea of a messiah (one who is "anointed") and a messianic kingdom is a significant feature of both Jewish and Christian beliefs. Those who study this issue point out that what is meant by these two terms has varied significantly over the centuries. Our attention here will focus on the development of Jewish ideas.

The concept of a messiah ruling over an ideal messianic kingdom was minimal in Jewish thought from the earliest days until Assyria's conquest of Israel. The focus rather was on God's direct rule over the nation in eternal righteousness. Following Israel's conquest, the prophet Isaiah began to introduce the idea of a messiah and his kingdom established in Zion, inhabited by the righteous remnant. It was in that context that there emerged the view of the messiah coming from king David's line. During the Babylonian exile, Isaiah's views were further developed through the prophets Jeremiah and Ezekiel.

The continued rule of foreigners over God's people only served to increase the Jews' longing for a messiah/deliverer. When the Maccabees and Hasmoneans overthrew the Syrians, messianic expectations greatly increased and the last century of the intertestamental era and the first Christian century were aglow with those hopes. The Maccabean and Hasmonean conquests over the Syrians had the dramatic effect of changing the Jews' view regarding the messiah. Simon Maccabee and John Hyrcanus of the Hasmoneans were both of the tribe of Levi, yet the Jews proclaimed them priest and king forever. When the Hasmoneans proved to be worldly and corrupt, the Jews once again looked to the Davidic line as the source for their messianic hopes.

During those years the Jews held a wide variety of views regarding the messiah and his kingdom. The Essenes looked for two messiahs — a military one and a religious one. Some saw him primarily as a military leader overthrowing the Romans; others viewed him as a prophet; still others looked for a priest/king. Many viewed the messianic kingdom as an earthly, political entity with Jerusalem as the capital, while others saw it as belonging to the heavenly realm.

Baptism. The origin of Christian baptism remains an unanswered question. No mention is made of baptism in the Old Testament; yet the opening pages of the New Testament assume it to be a common practice among Jews (Mark 1:4).

It is well known that washings have been practiced by many religions of the world from ancient times to the present. Those washings differ, however, in many ways from Christian baptism. A brief survey can be given regarding those differences.

Non-Christian baptism is usually referred to by a verb (to baptize), i.e., it is an action which is performed. It was normally self-administered as an initiation rite into a certain group or a rite of passage into one of the stages of life. That baptism or washing was done numerous times during the course of one's life and its purpose was to cleanse the body or soul from the stain of some wrong.

Christian baptism, on the other hand, is sometimes referred to by a verb, but more frequently by a noun (baptism), something which is an entity by itself. It is usually administered by an approved religious leader, and is an act of identification with the person of Jesus. It is normally performed only once and does not cleanse from wrong, since the New Testament teaches that that was done through the atoning work of Jesus (1 John 1:7).

Faint clues regarding the origin of Christian baptism come from three sources: intertestamental religious writings, the historian Josephus, and the Qumran community. These indicate that during the second century BC the Jews of Palestine and Syria began the practice of proselyte baptism. As the Jewish faith moved from Jerusalem to gentile lands, people were attracted to the faith and desired to become adherents to it. To meet the new development, Jewish leaders began to baptize proselytes.

The candidate was examined for his or her knowledge and practice of the Jewish faith. On successful completion of that examination, the candidate was self-immersed and thereby accepted into Judaism. Other than this general information, little is known of the beginnings of Christian baptism, but it is assumed that it developed from that Jewish practice.

The Cross. The cross as a means of execution was used in various parts of the world prior to the intertestamental era. References to death by crucifixion are found in Assyrian, Egyptian, Persian (cf. Ezra 6:11), Greek, Punic and Roman sources. Though the description of the physical appearance of the cross varied somewhat in different locales, its purpose remained the same — punishment and death.

The Old Testament prescribed death by hanging on a tree (Deut 21:23), but it appears that this was rarely done.

The first mention of the cross being used in the intertestamental era came during the reign of the Syrian king, Antiochus IV Epiphanes, who fomented the Maccabean revolt. The Jewish historian Josephus, who chronicled the Jewish wars with Rome, wrote of Antiochus's use of the cross (*Antiquities* 12.5.4).

The Romans then began to use the cross as a form of execution for slaves and criminals during the period of the republic, and during the period of the empire also crucified free men. This form of execution continued to be used by the Romans during the last century of the intertestamental era and the first two centuries of the Christian era. During those two hundred years hundreds of Christians were put to death on crosses.

Josephus wrote that death by crucifixion was a "most wretched way to die" (*Antiquities* 13.14.2; *Wars* 5.11.1). The victim was placed astride a peg which bore the body's weight, and the limbs were tied or nailed to a crossbar or main beam. In that helpless position the person waited to die, unable to move or ease the pain. At times death would take more than a day. During the New Testament period, Jewish leaders did not have the authority to execute a person, but could appeal to the Roman authorities to carry out an execution on the Sanhedrin's request.

4
CONCLUSION

Seven Reasons for the "Fullness of Time"

The reader will remember from the preface that a statement by St. Paul in his letter to the Galatians prompted the writing of this book. That statement said in effect that Jesus' birth came in the fullness of time, or at the right time in God's plan to save the world from sin and death. The political and religious developments of the four hundred years from the end of the Old Testament era until the birth of Jesus were surveyed in hopes of finding clues that might reveal why the time he was born was the right time in God's sight. Though it is risky to speak authoritatively about a subject on which the Bible is silent, one can piece together some reasons for God's decision based on the human events which occurred during the intertestamental years. The following are reasons which seem plausible, but it must be emphasized that they are only educated guesses by the writer. Seven reasons — four social and three religious — seem evident.

The first of the social reasons could be called the internationalism of the times. After Israel was destroyed by the Assyrians and Judah fell victim to Babylon, the Jewish faith moved out of the narrow confines of Palestine into the larger world. Either because of forced or voluntary migration, the Jews found themselves in many gentile lands. Because of this, their religion became known to the gentiles. Many of these simply learned about it, but others became adherents through baptism. When Alexander the Great appeared on the scene, he forged new relationships among Near Eastern, European, and Asian nations—an event which served to increase the sense of internationalism in the world. This opening up of the world helped to make the later coming of Christianity an international movement also.

The second social reason had to do with Alexander's introduction of Greek as the common language of the empire. With the Hebrew Bible translated to Greek and the writings of the early church also in Greek, large numbers of people were able to read that literature. Many responded to its message.

The third social reason was the development of a system of roads which tied the sprawling empire together. Alexander the Great began the process of building the roads, and the Romans substantially enlarged the network. Though dangers beset travelers, those roads did provide an important means of reaching many parts of the empire. This enabled Christian missionaries to travel far and wide in their effort to promote their religion.

The fourth social reason had to do with emperor Caesar Augustus's policy, known as "Pax Romana," the "Roman Peace." During the last years of the republic, the breakdown of social order was widespread. The various provinces which made up the republic frequently warred among themselves, inequities of justice among them prevailed, pirates raided seagoing vessels, the highways were infested with bandits, and corruption was an everyday fact. That deteriorating condition was the source of much unrest in the republic.

When Augustus became emperor, he reorganized the provinces along common rules, rid the sea of pirates, made the highways safer for travel, and in general brought peace and order to society. This was accomplished through his skillful organizational abilities and an army of half a million men which enforced the new rules. He believed that peace and order was necessary to govern that vast empire, and his army ensured its success. This orderly condition made it possible for the early missionaries to move across the empire using the road system with greater safety and effectiveness.

The first of the three religious reasons which may have prepared the world for the birth of Jesus was the translation of the Hebrew Bible into Greek. An important message of the Old Testament was that a messiah was to come. The Jews were already familiar with that message and many eagerly awaited him. With access to that scripture, the gentiles were then able to know it and to join in that anticipation. Many saw the fulfillment of that message in the life and person of Jesus.

The second reason may have been the introduction of the cross into Roman society. As we noted earlier, hanging on a tree was decreed as a form of capital punishment in Jewish society, though it was infrequently used. It was not until the last two centuries of the intertestamental era that death by hanging on a cross came to be used. The Syrian king Antiochus IV introduced it and the Romans adopted it and used it for about the first two centuries AD.

The significance of the cross at Jesus' birth can be seen in an interesting remark which Jesus himself made (Luke 24:26-27). He appears to be saying that even the manner of his death was foretold (John 3:14-15). If his death was to be "according to the scripture" (1 Cor 15:4) it would, this writer believes, have had to be associated with a cross in some form. The period of time in Palestine when that could have taken place was generally during that late intertestamental and early Christian era. It was "the window of opportunity" to fulfill that condition.

The third and last religious reason which may have contributed to the timing of Jesus's birth may be seen in St. Paul's letter regarding the purpose of the divine law in human redemption. In his letter to the Galatians, Paul taught that the divine law, for all of its truth and splendor, was a teacher, not a savior. The law taught the spiritual and moral will of God for all humanity, but it also was true that no one ever fully met its conditions or ever could.

Following that gloomy assessment, Paul continued with a hopeful word saying that inability to keep the divine law pointed to a way by which its just requirements could be met—that was faith in Jesus.

Paul appears to be saying that the giving of the divine law was not an end in itself, but a part of the divine plan to save the world. The stage for the law was completed and the next stage, the coming of Jesus to fulfill the law's requirements on behalf of humanity, was present. The final stage in that plan was yet to be revealed—the stage of fulfillment in eternal life, the ultimate purpose of the divine plan.

There has been a two-fold purpose in writing this book. One was to introduce the reader to the political and religious developments of the intertestamental years, showing that those years were not isolated or disconnected ones, but a vital link in the ongoing stories of Jewish and Christian history. It is hoped that this introduction will spur some to continue reading some of the many fine books available on the subject. The other purpose has been to explore what factors of that era contributed to the timing of Jesus' birth. For it is the conviction of the Christian community that it was not accidental, but part of the divine plan. The reader may or may not agree with the writer's view that the seven above named reasons contributed to the timing of Jesus' birth, but it is hoped that this book will also stimulate reflection on that issue.

APPENDIX A
SOURCES OF INFORMATION

Following are the primary sources of information regarding the intertestamental era as well as translations and secondary sources of information in English.

Scripture and Religious Writings:

The Septuagint: The Greek translations of the Old Testament made around 250 BC in Alexandria Egypt. It includes the Apocrypha.

The Apocrypha: Fifteen Jewish works written between 250 BC and 100 AD in Egypt and Palestine in Greek, Hebrew, and Aramaic. These works ultimately were rejected by the Jews as Scripture, but included in Roman Catholic Bibles. Later also in English translations of the Bible.
See Brenton, Lancelot C. L. *The Septuagint with Apocrypha: Greek and English*. Peabody, MA: Hendrickson, 1986. Note: The Apocrypha is included in most modern versions of the Bible.

Dead Sea Scrolls: Numerous copies of scripture and religious teachings from the Qumran community.
See Vermes, G. *The Dead Sea Scrolls in English*. 3rd ed. New York: Viking Penguin Inc., 1987.

The Midrashim: Commentaries and interpretations of scripture by various rabbis.

The Talmud: The Mishna, a record of oral traditions of the rabbis on various subjects. The Gemara, a collection of various interpretations of it.
For Midrash and Talmud, see Barrett, C. K. *The New Testament Background: Selected Documents*. Rev. San Francisco: Harper & Row, 1989.

Ancient Histories:

Flavius Josephus: Jewish historian contemporary with St. Paul. See
                     The Complete Works of Josephus. 4 vols. Grand
                     Rapids: Baker Book House, 1981.

Philo Judaeus: Jewish philosopher and historian from
                     Alexandria, Egypt. Contemporary with Jesus.
                     For Josephus and Philo, see Kee, Howard Clark.
                     *The Origins of Christianity: Sources and
                     Documents*. Englewood Cliffs, NJ: Prentice-Hall,
                     Inc., 1973. See also, Glatzer, Nahum N. *The
                     Essential Philo*. NY: Schocken Books, 1971.

Archaeology:

Tablet inscriptions: See Barrett, above.

Coins: See Banks, F. *Coins of Bible Days*. Long Island
                     City, NY: S. J. Durst, 1985. Also, Price, Martin
                     Jessop. *Coins and Their Cities: Architecture on the
                     Ancient Coins of Greece, Rome, and Palestine*.
                     Detroit: Wayne State University, 1977.

Papyrus: See Barrett, above.

Excavated Cities: See Mazar, Amahai. *Archaeology of the Land of
                     the Bible*. Anchor Reference Library. New York:
                     Doubleday, 1990. Also, Yamauchi, Edwin M.
                     *New Testament Cities in Western Asia Minor: Light
                     from Archaeology on Cities of Paul and the Seven
                     Churches of Revelation*. Grand Rapids: Baker
                     Book House, 1980.

APPENDIX B

Suggested Reading

BOOKS:

Albright, William F. *The Biblical Period From Abraham to Ezra: A Historical Survey*. New York: Harper & Row, 1963.

Ancient Egypt. Washington, D.C.: National Geographic Society, 1978.

Banks, F. *Coins of Bible Days*. Long Island City, NY: S. J. Durst, 1985.

Barrett, C. K. *The New Testament Background: Selected Documents*. Rev. & expan. San Francisco: Harper & Row, 1989.

Blair, Edward P. *Abingdon Bible Handbook*. Rev. Ed. Nashville: Abingdon, 1982.

Brenton, Lancelot C. L. *The Septuagint with Apocrypha: Greek and English*. Peabody, MA: Hendrickson, 1986.

Bruce, F. F. *New Testament History*. Garden City, NY: Doubleday, 1972.

Cate, Robert L. *A History of Bible Lands in the Interbiblical Period*. Nashville: Broadman, 1989.

The Complete Works of Josephus. 4 vols. Grand Rapids: Baker Book House, 1981.

Everyday Life in Bible Times. Rev. ed. Washington, D.C.: National Geographic Society, 1977.

Finegan, Jack. *The Archaeology of the New Testament: The Life of Jesus and the Beginning of the Early Church*. Princeton: Princeton University, 1969.

Foerster, Werner. *From the Exile to Christ: A Historical Introduction to Palestinian Judaism*. Trans. by Gordon E. Harris. Philadelphia: Fortress, 1964.

Frank, Harry T. & James F. Strange. *Discovering the Biblical World*.
        Rev. Ed. Maplewood, NJ: Hammond Inc., 1987.
Glatzer, Nahum N. *The Essential Philo*. NY: Schocken Books, 1971.
Greece and Rome: Builders of our World. Washington, D.C.: National
        Geographic Society, 1968.
Kee, Howard Clark. *The Origins of Christianity: Sources and
        Documents*. Englewood Cliffs, NJ: Prentice-Hall, 1973.
Kuntz, J. Kenneth. *The People of Ancient Israel: An Introduction to
        Old Testament Literature, History, and Thought*. New York:
        Harper & Row, 1974.
Lohse, Eduard. *The New Testament Environment*. Trans. by John E.
        Steely. Nashville: Abingdon, 1976.
Metzger, Bruce M. *Introduction to the Apocrypha*. New York:
        Oxford University, 1957.
_____*The New Testament: Its Background, Growth and Content*.
        Enl. Ed. Nashville: Abingdon, 1965.
Noth, Martin. *The Old Testament World*. Philadelphia: Fortress,
        1966.
Price, Martin Jessop. *Coins and Their Cities: Architecture on the
        Ancient Coins of Greece, Rome, and Palestine*. Detroit:
        Wayne State University, 1977.
Reicke, Bo. *The New Testament Era: The World of the Bible from 500
        B.C. to A.D. 100*. Minneapolis: Augsburg Fortress, 1974.
Russell, D. S. *Between the Testaments*. Minneapolis: Augsburg
        Fortress, 1960.
Vermes, G. *The Dead Sea Scrolls in English*. 3rd ed. New York:
        Viking Penguin, 1987.
Yamauchi, Edwin M. *New Testament Cities in Western Asia Minor:
        Light From Archaeology on Cities of Paul and the Seven
        Churches of Revelation*. Grand Rapids: Baker Book House,
        1980.

ARTICLES:

Andronicos, Manolis. "Regal Treasures From a Macedonian Tomb [Philip II, father of Alexander the Great] *National Geographic* (July, 1978): 55-77.

Boyer, David S. "Jerusalem to Rome in the Path of St. Paul," *National Geographic* (December, 1956): 707-59.

Field, Henry. "Sinai Sheds New Light on the Bible," *National Geographic* (December, 1948): 795-815.

LaFay, Howard, "Where Jesus Walked," *National Geographic* (December, 1967): 739-81.

"The Living Dead Sea," *National Geographic* (February, 1978): 225-45 [Dead Sea Scrolls].

MacLeish, Kenneth, "The Land of Galilee," *National Geographic* (December, 1965): 832-65.

Schreider, Helen & Frank, "In the Footsteps of Alexander the Great," *National Geographic* (January, 1968): 1-65.

Shanks, Hershel. "The Qumran Settlement," *Biblical Archaeology Review* 19 (May/June, 1993): 62-65.

Speiser, E. A., "Ancient Mesopotamia: A Light That Did Not Fail," *National Geographic* (January, 1951): 41-105.

Tushingham, A. Douglas, "The Men Who Hid the Dead Sea Scrolls," *National Geographic* (December, 1958): 785-808.

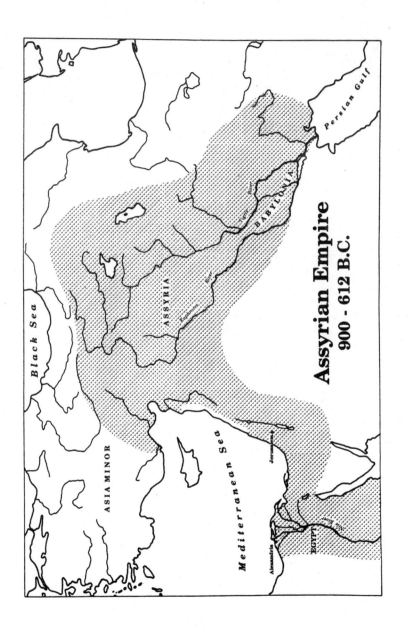

Assyrian Empire
900 - 612 B.C.

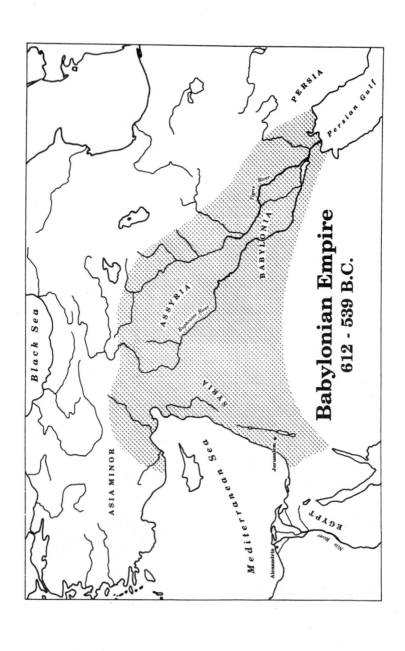

Babylonian Empire
612 - 539 B.C.

PERSIA

Persian Gulf

Tigris River

BABYLONIA

ASSYRIA

Euphrates River

SYRIA

Black Sea

ASIA MINOR

Mediterranean Sea

Jerusalem

EGYPT

Nile River

Alexandria

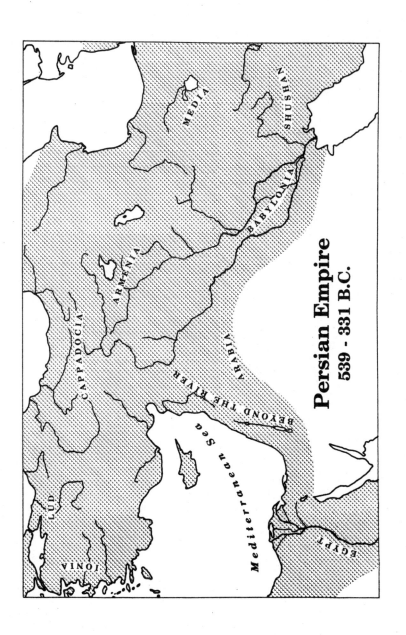

Persian Empire
539 - 331 B.C.

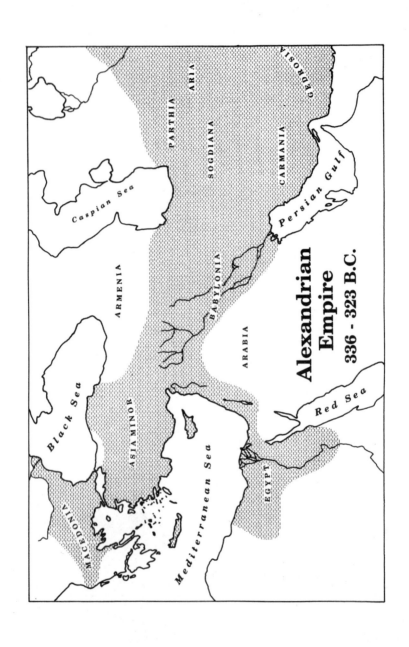

Alexandrian Empire
336 - 323 B.C.

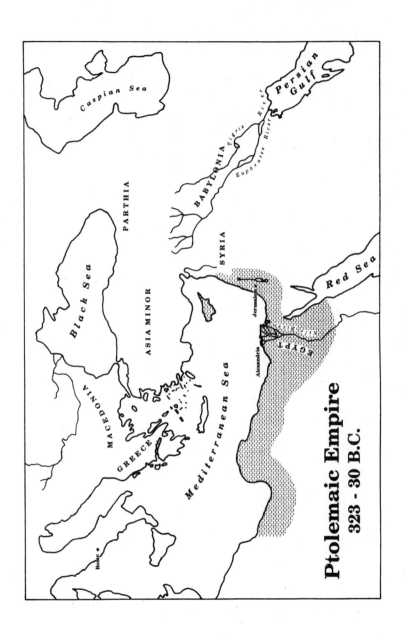

Ptolemaic Empire
323 - 30 B.C.

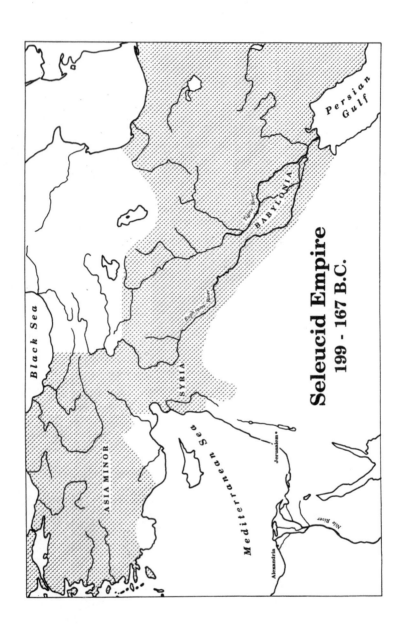

Seleucid Empire
199 - 167 B.C.

Persian Gulf

Black Sea

BABYLONIA

Tigris River

Euphrates River

SYRIA

ASIA MINOR

Mediterranean Sea

Jerusalem

Alexandria

Nile River

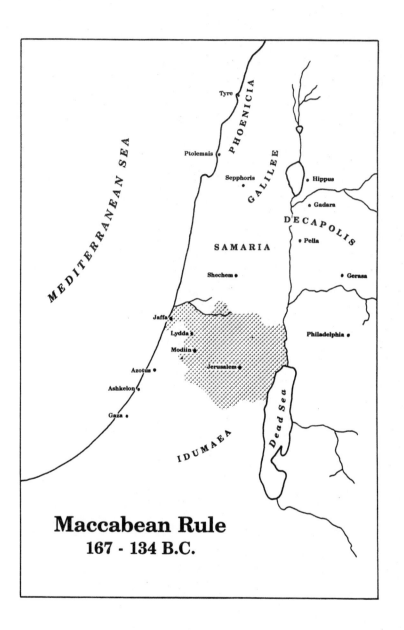

Tyre

PHOENICIA

Ptolemais

MEDITERRANEAN SEA

Sepphoris

GALILEE

Hippus

Gadara

DECAPOLIS

SAMARIA

Pella

Shechem

Gerasa

Jaffa

Lydda

Philadelphia

Modiin

Azotus

Jerusalem

Ashkelon

Dead Sea

Gaza

IDUMAEA

Maccabean Rule
167 - 134 B.C.

SYRIA

PHOENICIA

Tyre

Gush Halav

Ptolemais

GALILEE

Gamla

Hippus

Sepphoris

Yarmuk River

Geba

Gadara

Beth-shean

Pella

SAMARIA

Mediterranean Sea

Samaria

Shechem

Gerasa

Jabbok River

Jordan River

Jaffa

Lydda

Modiin

Philadelphia

Jabneh

Jericho

Azotus

Jerusalem

Qumran

Bethlehem

Ashkelon

Hebron

JUDAEA

En-gedi

Dead Sea

Arnon River

Gaza

Masada

Hasmonean Rule
134 - 63 B.C.

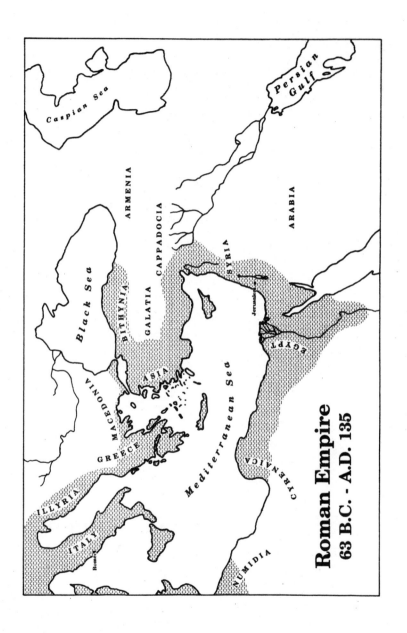

**Roman Empire
63 B.C. - A.D. 135**

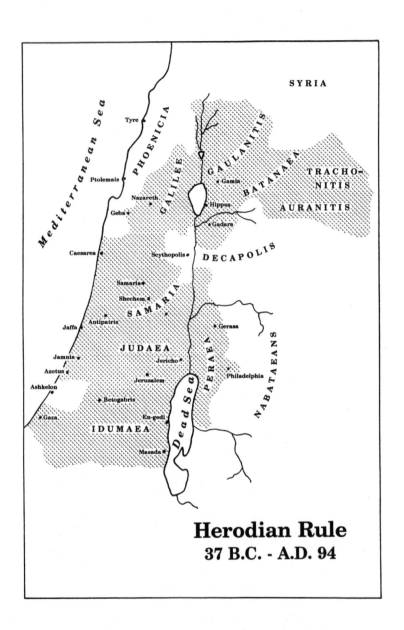

SYRIA

Mediterranean Sea

Tyre

PHOENICIA

GALILEE

GAULANITIS

BATANAEA

TRACHO-
NITIS

Ptolemais

Nazareth

Gamla

Hippus

AURANITIS

Geba

Gadara

Caesarea

Scythopolis

DECAPOLIS

Samaria

Shechem

SAMARIA

Jaffa

Antipatris

PERAEA

Gerasa

NABATAEANS

JUDAEA

Jamnia

Jericho

Azotus

Jerusalem

Philadelphia

Ashkelon

Betogabris

Dead Sea

Gaza

En-gedi

IDUMAEA

Masada

Herodian Rule
37 B.C. - A.D. 94

Other Titles Available from BIBAL Press